Making God
Part of Your Family
Volume 2

MAKING GOD PART OF { The FAMILY Bible Study Book } YOUR FAMILY

Volume 2

MICHAEL GRADY

NASHVILLE

NEW YORK • LONDON • MELBOURNE • VANCOUVER

Making God Part of Your Family

The Family Bible Study Guide - Volume 2

© 2019 Michael Grady

Published in New York, New York, by Morgan James Publishing. Morgan James is a trademark of Morgan James, LLC. www.MorganJamesPublishing.com

ISBN 9781642792492 paperback
ISBN 9781642792508 eBook
Library of Congress Control Number: 2018910470

Cover & Interior Design by:
Christopher Kirk
www.GFSstudio.com

Cover Artwork by:
Tyler Pate
tylerpate.designs@gmail.com

Morgan James is a proud partner of Habitat for Humanity Peninsula and Greater Williamsburg. Partners in building since 2006.

Get involved today! Visit
MorganJamesPublishing.com/giving-back

DEDICATION

The first time I met Marjorie Underwood, my mother-in-law to be, she told me very clearly what she thought her daughter needed in a husband. I was bold enough to question her ideas; apparently, this was what Marjorie wanted to hear. She challenged me to do right by her daughter, who soon became my beloved wife, Nan.

Even though our times together were not extensive, Marjorie and I developed a strong connection, which grew into mutual respect and, in time, admiration for each other. But when Nan and I moved from North Carolina to South Carolina, our connection was severed. I was responsible for breaking the bond with Marjorie. I let her down and I knew it; but I never found a way to mend it.

However, life with God is full of wonderful blessings and surprises. When Nan gave her mother a copy of Volume 1 of *Making God Part of Your Family*, Marjorie consumed it. She was excited. To use her words, "I finally have a clear understanding of the Bible and God's message. I now know he has a plan for us and, more specifically, for me." God used my book to re-establish our connection. She eagerly shared my book with everyone she encountered in the assisted-living home where she resides.

Approximately once a month, Marjorie reminds me to bring more books for her to give to people. I am impressed that Marjorie, who is now in her eighties, has established a new ministry. I am honored that God is allowing my book to be used as her method of witnessing. Thank you, Marjorie; you have been an inspiration and encouragement to me.

And it is my privilege to dedicate Volume 2 of *Making God Part of Your Family* to my mother-in-law, Marjorie Blanchard Underwood.

TABLE OF CONTENTS

Acknowledgments

My church family was so supportive and encouraging of my first book, *Making God Part of Your Family*, that I used their feedback extensively for this second volume. This is particularly true of my Bible study group that has been meeting weekly for thirty-three years. As a result, I would like to give them credit for helping me better communicate God's message regarding some of the more difficult to explain events discussed in Volume 2.

In addition, I would like to thank two ladies I work with, JoAnna Hicks and Andrea Graham; Andrea, for giving so much of her free time to provide editorial input, and JoAnna, for afterhours help in so many areas, including critical reviews, marketing, website creation, and helping me solve my most difficult task: gaining credibility in the Christian literary community as a former CPA turned author.

I would also like to thank my wife, Nan, for her constant support and contributions. More important, I thank her because she sees this as "our" project to minister to the family of God.

Once again, I am very grateful to Free Bible Images (www.freebibleimages. org) for the generous contribution of their illustrations in this book. It is important for families to have a visual image as they read and listen to the truths presented in each story.

Finally, I would like to acknowledge Dr. M. R. DeHaan, who founded the Radio Bible Class—now, Our Daily Bread Ministries—for his Old Testament Bible Studies that have had a lasting influence on my understanding of God's message to us.

Many of the Bible quotes in this book are my own paraphrase to assist in the ease of reading the story.

INTRODUCTION

Making God Part of Your Family, Volume 2, continues retelling the stories of the Old Testament. The primary purpose of this series is to bring to life God's plan for you and your family as he chose to reveal it through his people in the Old Testament. Hopefully, through the insights I share, you will understand that these stories are much more than a history of the Israelites (God's Chosen Family). The stories are also parables detailing God's guide to living life while on this earth and his eternal plan for redemption and salvation for all who choose to join him. God has a message that will be truly life changing if we take the time to read and listen to his Word.

In today's world the family is confronted with an onslaught of conflicting and unhealthy messages, much like the families in the Old Testament. Over the last few decades, our culture has experienced a complete shift in morals and beliefs, making it more important than ever to understand the benefits of having a loving God and the support of a close-knit family to lean on. If you are not fortunate enough to have a blood family, you can still accept God's invitation to join him and his people, a family known as the body of Christ (the church universal).

In contrast to the world's standards, the stories presented in Volume 2 will teach the importance of kindness and putting the needs of others ahead of our own. These stories also highlight the strength that comes through unity and working together. It is important to acknowledge that modern families can be very broken; in turn, they may not provide the love, wisdom, and rich relationships God intended to provide for us through the family unit. These stories demonstrate how we, as Christians, need to be understanding and offer support to those around us who need love, compassion, and guidance.

When we accept God's invitation to join his family, Jesus and all his followers become our family, too (including Adam and Eve, Moses, Abraham, and the Chosen Family of Israel). Regardless of whom our earthly family is, we can experience how God, our Father, loves us perfectly and will always guide us in perfect wisdom. Jesus is not only our Savior and God but also our brother. He sacrificed himself so we can be fully part of his family and share his inheritance.

I am praying these stories will help each of us strengthen our family as we examine the successes and failures of our biblical patriarchs. It is my hope this family theme, being "part of God's family," will provide you with the resources you need to become an effective and valuable member of God's family.

For over thirty years, I taught Sunday school and Bible studies for adults, teenagers, and eight- to twelve-year-olds. Most Christians admit the need to have a stronger knowledge of the Bible. However, when asked why they spend very little time reading God's Word, the answer is consistently the same:

- The Bible is too hard to understand.
- Too much of the Bible is boring.
- The Old Testament is not relevant.

I hope to change these misconceptions by retelling the Old Testament stories, making them more engaging and easier to understand, often tying the Old and New Testament together. You will soon see how relevant these stories really are, both to our daily lives and to our eternal relationship with God and Jesus Christ. Jesus used parables to teach us principles of life, and in the same way, the stories in the Old Testament guide and assist us through the trials, tribulations, and joys of this life while also preparing us for eternity. Although these stories may not call him by name, they do paint beautiful portraits of Jesus, the source of our salvation and redemption.

A Family Bible Study Book: Not Just a Storybook

If you have been looking for a way to read the Bible to your children or with your family while providing interest to a variety of age groups, this book may be your answer. Most Bible storybooks are oriented toward young children, making them too simplistic for adults and teenagers to enjoy. On the other hand, those written as Bible study books are often too difficult for children and most teenagers to understand.

These stories are a unique combination; they are both basic enough for children to understand and deep enough to help parents and older family members grow in the knowledge and wisdom of God's Word. Accordingly, this book is written on an adult level but structured so that it can be read and discussed together with younger family members. The stories have a conversational tone to facilitate discussions. Children who are eight to twelve years old are unlikely to fully understand the messages if they read the stories on their own, but if read together with a parent, grandparent, or Sunday school teacher, the young reader is quite capable of understanding the primary message. This idea expresses my main purpose for writing this series: that the family spends time together reading and understanding the Bible. In addition, I have been pleased that teenagers and young adults have found the messages particularly relevant. They have said, "Finally, I understand what the Old Testament is about and why it is so important," and "I am intrigued with how much depth you provided in each story, but at the same time, you made it so much easier to understand."

So even though this book retells stories from the Bible, it is not just a Bible storybook. It is a study book in small, thought-provoking doses. In that vein, my experience in reading these stories to and with elementary-age children and teenagers has shown that thirty to forty-five minutes is a good amount of time to set aside for reading and discussing each story. However, the book can also be used for a ten- to fifteen-minute nightly devotion with older elementary-aged children (eight- to twelve-year-olds) or as an in-depth study for mature Christians who want to dig deeper into God's Word by seeking out the scriptures provided at the end of each story.

Whether you use these stories to structure an in-depth family discussion, read with your children at bedtime, or take the time for personal Bible study and later share what you have learned, your family will:

- Develop a better and deeper understanding of God, our Father, and his Son, Jesus
- Learn how we are part of God's family
- Learn how God expects us to live amidst the joys and sorrows of life
- Apply practical lessons and eternal truths to the situations we face today

Bible Background: Setting the Stage

As stated in the Introduction in Volume 1, the Bible (the Word) is God's message to all people. Through his Word, we find that his message begins and ends with the revelation of Jesus Christ—that is, God telling us who Jesus is. Within each of the Bible stories, God is sharing the following with us:

- Human history from beginning to end (our family history)
- A guide to living our lives on earth
- Most important, for us, who God is and his plan of salvation

The Old Testament is divided into three main sections: (1) History and the Law, (2) Poetry and Wisdom, and (3) the Prophets. However, all of the books point to Jesus, God's Son. Jesus, in his teachings, tells us that the entire Old Testament is a book of prophecy, or messages from God about the future. Jesus told the religious leaders of his day that Moses wrote about him, confirming that Genesis is a book of prophecies and picture-stories that show us who Jesus is. Jesus further instructs us that the Psalms and other Old Testament books talk about his life and how he will save us. These pronouncements of Jesus are affirmed by Paul and other authors of the New Testament books.

Portraits of Christ

Prophecies are revealed as God provides the history of mankind through his Word. We see pictures, and at times more formal portraits, of Jesus hidden in the Old Testament stories of the patriarchs, the ancient fathers of God's family. In these pictures, not only do we see Jesus, but we also learn of God's plan to rescue us. Further, we learn through these stories how God is calling us to live *his* way. Many of these revelations are shrouded in mystery until they are revealed in the New Testament; some we still may not understand. Thankfully, the New Testament writers shed light upon these Old Testament stories, and through their revelations we see how God's plans were first revealed in the stories of the patriarchs.

The pictures that God draws for us in the Old Testament come in varying shapes, sizes, and nuances. Some are bold and clear, such as the picture of Abraham sacrificing his son Isaac as an incredible symbol of God sacrificing his own Son for us. Other portraits are like silhouettes, making it somewhat difficult to determine who is in the picture. But as we get to know our Savior better and better, the silhouettes become an undeniable picture God painted for us.

For example, suppose someone who does not know me very well were shown a silhouette of my daughter. This person would not be able to tell you who she is and certainly would not know much about her. But someone who has spent time with me and my family would easily recognize my daughter and call her by name. And so, it is with our Old and New Testament readings. The more intimate we become with them, the clearer the pictures become—even if some are still in mystery form. With a deeper study of the Bible, we are able to understand the pictures God has drawn for us—and we begin to see a portrait of how we are to live.

So why has God chosen to speak in images and mysteries instead of being more direct? The disciples asked Jesus, "Why do you speak in parables?" His response was that he wanted us to study his stories. Those who thought the stories were foolish or unimportant would miss the true meaning and ignore them. Only those who were truly interested in him would take the time to understand. By opening our eyes and ears to God's Word, we discover the stories' meaning, and the Holy Spirit guides us in this endeavor. The Holy Spirit is God in spirit form, sent to live within the hearts of all those who believe that Jesus died and rose again for us.

How True Are These Stories?

Okay, so we are given these stories to show us who God is and his plan for us. But are they just pictures and stories, or are they about real people? In the Gospels, Jesus speaks of the men, women, and children of the Old Testament as real people who lived in history. A few examples may help. He said, *"Just as it happened* in the days of Noah, so shall it be in the days of the Son of Man." He told others, "Before Abraham was born, I am." He even talks about stories that are hard to believe, such as when he said, "It was the same *as happened* in the days of Lot . . . [He] went out from Sodom, and it rained fire and brimstone . . . It will be the same in the day that the Son of Man is revealed . . . Remember Lot's wife, who was turned into a pillar of salt." And finally, *"Just as* Jonah was three days and three nights in the belly of the fish, so will the Son of Man be three days and three nights in the heart of the earth." Jesus compares his personal life events with sensational and sometimes hard to believe Old Testament stories. Jesus claims his upcoming events were *just as* real as these Old Testament stories. Therefore, if Jesus spoke of these ancestors as real people, why shouldn't we? However, whether or not you believe these stories were historical events will not change the important practical applications they will provide to you and your family or the message that God reveals regarding his plan for all of us.

How to Use This Book

If you are reading this book in a family setting, I encourage you to read the stories out loud. Feel free to pause in the middle of each reading to discuss a specific point or to relate the story to an event or situation in your family's life; thus, you will allow these stories to become your family stories. Following each story are two sections providing for additional discussion and research. The first section includes questions and comments for further discussion, to help the details of the story penetrate more deeply into your lives. The second section includes notes and references to other related passages in the Bible so that your family can learn more about the meaning and significance behind certain parts of the story. Feel free to look up and read these references together, depending on the age, needs, and interests of your family.

It's not enough to receive these stories as your own family history; we should also accept that they are the Word of God written to each of us. God has given you the gift of the Bible to help you develop a close relationship with him and to give you instruction and comfort in every circumstance of your life—whether significant and overwhelming or seemingly unimportant. My hope is that each time you read this book, not only will you find new details that were previously unseen, but even more important, you will also grow, both together as a family and in your personal relationship with God.

A Note about Volume 2

While having a few test groups read a draft of Volume 2, one consistent message came through that at first surprised me. Many people said these stories reach a deeper level than those in Volume 1. While that was not necessarily my intention, after reflecting on this input, I realized it's the way God provided the stories. Many of the stories in Volume 2 are difficult to take in as they relate to the harsher realities of life:

- Why does God instruct the Israelites to kill women and children along with the enemy soldiers?
- Is the God of the Old Testament different than the God of the New Testament?
- How could the Israelites have witnessed so many miracles and yet be so disobedient to God?
- How could God's people be so sinful, violent, and disrespectful, both to him and to each other?
- When the Israelites were worshipping God properly, why were they sometimes having difficulties?
- Does God really let Satan have his way with us? Does Satan really rule this world? Will Satan's rule end?
- Is it really necessary for us to suffer the trials and tribulations of this life to experience God?
- Why does God say that doing what is right in our own eyes is inconsistent with his ways?

All of these questions and more are addressed in the retelling of the stories in this volume, which covers the Old Testament books of Joshua, Judges, Ruth, Job, and 1 Samuel.

Chapter 1

Joshua Leads the Israelites into the Promised Land

Joshua 1–5

At the conclusion of *Making God Part of Your Family, Volume 1*, we left God's people wandering in the wilderness. The Israelites had been too afraid to enter the Promised Land because the enemy was too strong, or so they thought. They should have known that God would lead them to victory. God was so upset with them that he made them wander in the wilderness for forty years until all the men over twenty years old died—except for Joshua and Caleb. These two men were the only spies out of the twelve that Moses sent to check out their new homeland who said, "With God's help, we can conquer the land."

Joshua Takes over the Leadership of God's People

Before Moses died, he let the people of Israel know that God had chosen Joshua to take his place in leading the nation. When God was ready, he spoke to Joshua,

> *Arise, cross the Jordan River, for I am ready to give the land to my People. Just as I was with Moses, I will be with you. Be strong and courageous; I will not fail you nor forsake you.*

Joshua, in turn, told the Israelites to be prepared to serve the Lord. If they were willing to be obedient, God would bless them and give them the land he promised to their fathers. Wouldn't it be great to know that God will not fail you nor forsake any of your efforts? God is on our side, no matter how disobedient we are, and he loves us no matter what we do. But as Joshua shared in this story, God expects us to make a commitment to follow his commandments. When we fail, he calls us to repent. When we follow this pattern, he will not let us down.

The Israelites were excited yet apprehensive because they were not trained for battle. Was God really going to be there? At times, we all are afraid. What are you afraid of? Bugs? The dark? Failure? A boss? Cancer? God can help, and he will protect you, but you must draw near to him. Let's see how God helped the Israelites.

As the people were preparing to cross the Jordan River, Joshua sent two spies to check out the city of Jericho; this city would be the first battleground. Soon after the spies entered Jericho, they learned how frightened the people were of the two-million Israelites camped just on the other side of the river. The people of Jericho had heard of the mighty victories God had given his People during their journey from Egypt. Even though the events took place forty years earlier, they knew about the parting of the Red Sea and the destruction of the Egyptian army.

The spies found favor through a woman named Rahab. When the king learned they were staying with her, he sent his men to Rahab's home to capture the spies. Rahab told them that the spies left through the city gates although at that moment she was hiding them on her roof. When the men left the city to chase the spies, Rahab helped the two Israelites escape by letting them climb down a rope through a window in her house. She advised them to leave the city by heading into the hill country to hide from those searching for them.

Before the spies left, Rahab asked them to repay her kindness by saving her when they returned to take over Jericho; so, they told her to tie a scarlet ribbon on her door to identify her house. Then the two spies escaped, and after three days of hiding, they returned to Joshua to report all that happened. They shared

how frightened the people of Jericho were and told of Rahab's good deed. Joshua was excited to learn the people were frightened and declared, "Surely the Lord has given all the land into our hands."

We are not specifically told why Rahab helped the spies; however, I believe she searched her heart and decided the God of the Israelites was the only true God. Thus, she made the choice to help the spies, even though all of her people served other gods. We may be faced with similar choices in our lives. We hear all around us, on TV and in the news, that Christian beliefs are foolish, and the commandments of God are not the right ones to follow. Can you name some instances of TV shows that are disrespectful toward or laugh at God's ways?

Could you be as brave as Rahab and choose to be on God's side, even though you could get in trouble for doing so? What if the men she hid had been found on her roof? What if they were later caught and confessed that she had helped them? Our choices will not always be easy, but Rahab was rewarded greatly for making the right choice. Not only were she and her family saved when the Israelites came to destroy Jericho, but also, we later learn that she married Salmon, a descendant of Judah.[1] Together, they had a son who was an ancestor of King David and Jesus. What a glorious prize for choosing God when no one else around her did! How would it make you feel to be one of the direct ancestors of Jesus?

Ark of the Covenant

While the Israelites waited on the east side of the Jordan River for the spies to report back, God shared his plans with Joshua. There was much to be done, and it would take a long time to get so many people ready to enter the Promised Land.

Many years before, God commanded Moses to construct a golden box with two angels facing each other on top of the box.[2] This beautiful box and its contents were to be reminders of God's promises to the Israelites. The box was kept in a tent called the Tabernacle, which was the place where Moses—and later, the priests—visited God. This box became known as the Ark of the Covenant; "covenant" means God's promise. The Ark was a reminder that his People served a mighty and powerful God who performed miracles for them. The Ark that Moses built would be the centerpiece to lead the people across the River.

Inside the Ark were the following:[3]

- The stone tablets on which the Ten Commandments were inscribed by God himself;
- Aaron's wooden rod, which miraculously grew almonds, as a sign that his family would become the high priests of Israel;[4] and
- A piece of manna as a reminder of God's faithfulness to his Chosen People; manna was special bread provided by God for the Israelites each morning for the entire forty years they wandered in the wilderness. On

the day the Israelites crossed the Jordan River, the manna from heaven ceased because their new homeland was "flowing with milk and honey"

Crossing the Jordan

Now that the spies had reported back, and the priests were ready, Joshua commanded,

> *When you see the Ark of the Covenant being carried by the priests, then you will know that the journey has begun. However, as you follow the Ark, make sure that you do not come near it, for the power of the Lord is in the Ark.*

As the priests who were carrying the Ark stepped foot in the Jordan River, the water stopped flowing, thus allowing the Israelites to cross over on dry ground. This, of course, was a reminder of how God parted the Red Sea, and just as God was with Moses, he would be with Joshua as he led God's people into the Promised Land. Can you imagine what the people in the nearby cities thought? First, two million or more people were crossing into their land, and then they saw an even more frightening event: the water that flowed by their city backed up, creating a wall of water. The Bible says that their hearts melted and there was no spirit in them; that is, they no longer had any fight in them.

Do you think the people who lived upstream came out to see the spectacle? Or do you think they stayed inside their homes, trembling in fear for what God might do to them? God's judgment came for the inhabitants of this land just as one day God's judgment will come upon us. Are you are going to choose to be on his side now? Or are you going to tremble in fear, waiting for his judgment to come upon you? Now is the time to choose.

Once all of the Israelites crossed the Jordan River—but before the priests with the Ark exited the river—a person from each of the twelve tribes was instructed to take a large stone out of the river bed. With these twelve stones, Joshua built an altar on the banks of the river as a memorial for the sons of Israel to remind them that the Lord was with his people when they entered the Promised Land and would be there for them in the future.

We, too, need to build altars during our lifetime; or maybe you would better understand if I suggested that we build memories of times God intervened in our lives and made a difference. When we recount these events, the memory will be a reminder that it was God who helped us—not just luck or a twist of fate. We should keep these memories in a "treasure box" in our heart so that when we have troubled times, we can remember God is with us and will come to our rescue again. So that you will not forget, I suggest you write down these memories and reflect on them when you are having a difficult time hearing from God. Best of all, we can know that "once we cross the Jordan River," we will each receive our Promised Land: a "mansion" in heaven we can look forward to for eternity.[5] What memories are in your heart's "treasure box" for you to pull out in times of trouble?

On this day, the Israelites saw the power of God displayed and recognized that the Lord was now with Joshua. God honored him just as he had honored Moses before him. The people were now ready to follow Joshua; however, before the Lord would allow them to enter the battle, each male had to be circumcised. Why? During the years of wandering in the wilderness, the Israelites had failed to circumcise all male children, which was their part of the covenant that God made with Abraham, their "father," to be their God.

Our Own Battleground

The Israelites were freed from slavery when they left Egypt, but they would be required to fight before they would be able to live peacefully in the Promised Land. The Bible tells us that Satan is the ruler of this world and we must be ready.[6] We need to heed the commandments of God and worship him, just as the Israelites conformed to God's requirement for all males to be circumcised. Are there promises you made to God that have been long forgotten? Do you need God's forgiveness for something you have done? Do you need to forgive someone for something that was done to you? Or do you need to recognize that Jesus is your Savior and begin to follow him? Once we are right with God, we can join the battle. Our enemy is powerful, and we do not want to take the enemy lightly.

God gave us the plan we need to follow. In Paul's New Testament letter to the Ephesians, he tells us we are to "stand firm and put on the full armor of God." He compared God's armor to a soldier's armor of that day and said, "Our battle is *not* against our fellow human beings, but it is against the devil and his army of wicked angels in the heavenly places" (a spiritual world we cannot see). Finally, Paul said, "We are to be in prayer at all times."[7] Therefore, we are to submit to God. He will help us fight against our enemy, and the victory will be ours.

In our next two stories, we will see the battles that took place in the Promised Land. God gave the land to the Israelites, but not without a fight. God's people were free from slavery and ready to receive their reward of the Promised Land, but it would not come without trials and tribulations. When they were following God, his power prevailed. However, when they faltered and turned away from God, the enemy won the battle. As Christians, we, too, are free from the slavery of sin and are headed to our Promised Land (heaven). As with the Israelites, our journey will not be without battles and hardships along the way. However, when we are following God, we can know he is with us and the final victory will be worth all of the trials; our suffering will be amazingly rewarded. These Old Testament stories help teach us how to survive.

For Further Discussion
- Getting ready for battle is very important. Explain how getting ready God's way is different from the way you learn about in this world.
- Rahab put herself and her family at great risk when she hid the spies. What was her reward? Discuss how you can stand up for God and how that decision could hurt you now but will one day be rewarded.
- Are you ready to serve God in any way he chooses?

For Further Study
1. Matthew 1:5—Salmon was the father of Boaz, whose mother was Rahab.
2. Exodus 37:1–9—Bezalel made an ark and covered it with pure gold, with two cherub angels facing each other.
3. Hebrews 9:4—Inside the Ark were the tablets of the covenants, Aaron's rod that budded, and manna.
4. Numbers 17:1–8—A representative from all twelve tribes placed a rod in the tent of meeting, and it was Aaron's rod that budded into ripe almonds, showing his family was chosen to be the priestly family for Israel.
5. John 14:1–3—Do not be troubled. In my father's house are many mansions; I am going there to prepare a place for you.
6. John 12:31; 14:30—The ruler of this world (the devil) will be cast out because he can find nothing wrong in the life of Jesus.
7. Ephesians 6:10–18—Be strong in the Lord; put on his armor to fight the enemy (the devil) that lives in the spiritual world and comes into this world to harm you. Stand firm by putting on the full armor of God and cover it all with prayer.

Chapter 2
JOSHUA AT THE BATTLE OF JERICHO
Joshua 5–6

In our last story, Joshua was leading the Israelites into the Promised Land. But there were major battles to be fought before they could enjoy the fruits of the land and God's promises for peace and comfort. We, too, have battles we must face and an enemy to resist as we live and learn to serve our God and Savior, Jesus Christ. We are called to put on God's armor and stand firm. These battles are preparation for the final confrontation that will come at the time designated by God when he returns to take over this world, which mankind gave to Satan in the Garden of Eden. In the story of the Battle of Jericho, we see a picture of how the future battle will unfold; this story is a prophecy for the end times.

God's Battle Instructions

As Joshua was contemplating the upcoming battle, he saw a man standing with a sword as one ready for combat. Joshua asked, "Are you for us or for our adversaries?" The man replied, "I come now as a captain of the Lord of hosts." Realizing that he was confronted by an angel of God, Joshua fell on his face. The angel told Joshua to remove his sandals, for he was standing on holy ground. Do you remember that God spoke to Moses from the burning bush and told him the same thing?

Then the Lord spoke to Joshua, "I have given Jericho into your hands with its king and his valiant warriors." He gave Joshua specific instructions for the battle; the men of war, the priests carrying the Ark of the Covenant and seven more priests with trumpets were to march once around the city walls in total silence except for the seven priests who were to blow their trumpets. After they completed their march, they would return to camp, leaving the people in Jericho to wonder what would happen next.

9

Joshua was to follow the same procedure for six days. Then on the seventh day, the soldiers and the priests were to march around the city seven times. As they completed the seventh circle, the priests were to give one long horn blast. When the men heard the blast, they were to shout altogether with a great noise, and the walls of the city would fall flat allowing Joshua's warriors to attack and destroy all those inside.

God's instructions directed that no man, woman, or child was to be left alive—even the animals were to be killed. All the gold, precious jewels, and valuables would belong to the Lord; no one was to keep any of the spoils of victory. Because God was responsible for the victory, all the spoils would go into God's treasury. It was very important for God's instructions to be followed exactly; this was a test to ensure that God's Chosen Family would obey *all* of his instructions.

Understanding God's Ways

Before we read how the battle turned out, I think it will be helpful to discuss God's very troubling instructions. Why would God command that even the women and seemingly innocent children be killed? That does not sound like the God of love, mercy, and forgiveness we read about in the New Testament. This is a good time to explain that the stories in Volume 2 will frequently reveal difficult messages that stretch our beliefs and cause us to think outside of our comfort zone. I believe the best place to start with troubling truths is to recognize that God's ways are not our ways. In our human state, we are not capable of seeing and comprehending all of life's circumstances from his perspective.

Many times in the Bible, we are not told God's view of the people's actions, and at times, we see no direct discipline or consequence for their seemingly bad choices. In these instances, we are left to interpret God's instructions based on reading other passages in the Bible. Other verses may shed light on the story and enable us to understand, to the degree we can, the character of God. Accordingly, we should proceed with the knowledge that we serve our God, who is far more sympathetic and forgiving than we can comprehend, and learn to accept his judgment, even when we cannot understand his reasons.

As far as this passage is concerned, I offer the following as my explanation: we are not told how often God may have offered chances for these people to turn from their wicked ways. We know from the stories in Volume 1 that God tried diligently to get everyone to serve him. However, the human race developed a pattern of life that often excluded God; they were committed to pursuing their own selfish pleasures, and without realizing it, they served the god of this world (the devil). Therefore, God had no other choice but judgment, just as he will have no other choice when it comes to the "end times" and Jesus returns to reclaim this world for his Father. The judgment carried out on Jericho is a prophecy of that future event.

Time after time, we find in Scripture that God is just, fair, and willing to give chance after chance. If the children, who were killed under God's orders, were willing and capable of turning to him, then I believe he received them into his heavenly home. If they were too young to decide for themselves, he would not condemn them, and they, too, would be received into God's heavenly home. But he had to eliminate the possibility of these children intermarrying with the Israelites, thus infecting God's family with their inherent immoral and wicked behaviors. God had separated the Israelites from all other people of the world for the last four hundred years. He even permitted them to endure slavery to preserve the character and qualities he needed in a people who would serve the one true God. If he allowed these inhabitants of the Promised Land to become part of the family of God, all of his efforts to separate Israel would have been in vain.

And even more important to consider, we only think in terms of our anticipated eighty to ninety years on this earth, but God thinks in terms of eternity. So, from an eternal perspective, I believe God will give the people who were then residing in the Promised Land the same opportunity and consideration he gives to everyone else.

The Battle

When the day came for the battle with Jericho to begin, the armed men of war went first, followed by the seven priests who were blowing their trumpets; trailing them were the priests carrying the Ark of the Covenant. As Joshua commanded, no voice was heard; the trumpets provided the only sound as God's people marched around the city walls.

Imagine what was going on inside the city of Jericho that first day. As the spies explained, the people were already frightened, trembling at the thought of what might happen to them. And now to see an entire army marching in silence—what were they to think? The people kept waiting for an attack that did not come.

On the second day, the men of war once again marched around Jericho, followed by the priests carrying the Ark and blowing their trumpets; all was silent except for the haunting sound of seven trumpets. The third day, the same thing happened, and so it was for the first six days. Each day, the people of Jericho became more and more frightened. When would the attack occur? Why didn't they just get it over with?

On the seventh day, something changed. Once they completed their march around the city, Israel continued on a second time and then a third time. Now, what do you think was going on in the minds of the people of Jericho? For six days, the same thing had happened, and now something different was occurring. Can't you see them talking to their neighbors? Would this be the day? Would they survive the attack? It had to be a frightening time for the inhabitants of Jericho.

Finally, on the seventh march around the city, there was a loud, continual blast by the trumpeters; at the same time, Joshua called the soldiers to give a great shout. The noise was so loud that the walls of the city fell. And when "the walls of the city came tumbling down," the men of war were free to run straight into the city and attack the people of Jericho. By this time, the people were so frightened they couldn't respond, so the Israelites won without losing a single life. As God commanded, no one in Jericho survived except the family of Rahab, who had done as she was instructed and tied a scarlet ribbon on her door.

Do you remember Rahab? She helped the spies escape from the men of Jericho. As the Israelites attacked the city, the two spies were given instructions to retrieve Rahab and her family and escort them out of the city, thus fulfilling their promise. As I shared in the last story, Rahab became a valuable member of the Chosen Family.

How could people shouting cause a wall so thick and strong to simply come tumbling down? A number of years ago, there was a TV commercial with a lady

singing such a high note that it broke a glass. Could something similar have happened that day in Jericho? I'm sure it could have, but I like to think there was more at play than mere physics. We will learn in later stories that the angels of God helped the nation of Israel fight its battles. Once, the Bible even describes the angels in battle formation, ready to fight for the nation of Israel.[1] We will also learn that Michael, the archangel, was assigned as the military protector for the nation of Israel to fight against Satan and his angels.[2]

So even though it is not mentioned in the story, I like to think that God's army of angels was surrounding the city of Jericho. When the people shouted, the angels used some form of spiritual "sledgehammer" to slam against the walls, which caused them to tumble down. Of course, we do not know this; but remember, we were told that before the battle began, God sent an angel who looked like a warrior with his sword drawn and ready for combat. Therefore, I believe this angel cleared the path for the Israelites' entry into Jericho.

We are taught a great lesson from this battle; the power of God is available to us when we are committed to follow all of his instructions carefully and completely. In the next story, we will learn what happens when people do not follow God's instructions and how disobedience hinders God's people. As I write these stories, this very thing is happening in the United States. So many people are no longer following God's instructions, even many who actively participate in church. And often, Christians choose to believe what they think is right, instead of following the Word of God.

We have allowed society and our friends to influence what we believe is right. As a result, we have lost the power of God that is available to us because we are not committed to follow *all* of his instructions. Let's take this opportunity to examine how we are living our lives and how we often let others dictate what is right and wrong, rather than turning to God for direction. I challenge you to take time each day to learn more about God's Word and to become more committed to following God's direction. If we do, I believe we will see God's power active on earth once again.

Prophecy for End Times

At the beginning of this story, I shared that the Battle of Jericho was a prediction of the final battle between God and his enemy, Satan. Let's see what insight this Old Testament battle can give us into God's plan for what the Bible calls the end times. The term "end times" means the end of Satan's rule on earth, the time when God comes to reclaim the earth for his people. With God leading the way, Joshua and the Israelites reclaimed the Promised Land that had been taken over by the Canaanites, the Philistines, and the other people of the land. In the same way, God will return and call upon his army to take over this world that is rightfully his.

I see a remarkable comparison between the Battle of Jericho and the New Testament description of the end times, particularly passages in Revelation, the last book of the Bible. Revelation describes seven sealed judgments that will be poured out on the earth. As described in this book of the Bible, when it came time to open the seventh seal, there were seven trumpets of judgments.[3] Can you begin to see the correlation? The daily marches around Jericho symbolically represent each of the first six sealed judgments leading up to the final battle that Revelation calls Armageddon.[4] The seven times the army circled around Jericho on the seventh day are like the seven trumpets of judgment that will come out of the seventh seal in Revelation. Notice that the priests carried *seven* trumpets in their march around Jericho. And there is more.

These events led up to the attack in the Battle of Jericho, and similarly the events described in Revelation will lead to the battle to reclaim the earth at Armageddon. It is interesting to note that the seven judgments coming out of the seventh seal were identified by trumpets. The shouts of the army of Israel, the loud blast of the trumpets after the seventh circle around Jericho, and the destruction of the city compare to the end times described in the New Testament when Jesus returns. First Thessalonians 4 says,

For the Lord himself will descend from heaven with a shout, with the voice of the archangel and with the trumpet of God.[5]

With the coming of the Lord, the final battle of Armageddon begins. John writes of this in Revelation 19:

And I saw heaven opened and behold a white horse and he who sat on it was called Faithful and True and in righteousness he judges and wages war . . . and the armies which are in heaven, clothed in fine linen, white, were following him on white horses . . . And I saw the beast and the kings of the earth and their armies assembled to make war against him who sat on the horse and against his army. And the beast and the false prophet were seized . . . and the rest were killed with the sword.[6]

So, beginning with the sound of the trumpet and the shouts of the army of God, the victory is God's—both at Jericho and Armageddon. Like the inhabitants of Jericho, those on earth and those in Satan's army will have no chance against the Lord's army at Armageddon. The battle will be over before it begins.

Jesus will seize the beast and the false prophet and throw them into the lake of fire as punishment for their deeds, and those who worship false gods will be killed with the sword. No one will be spared.

God's faithful servants are to be ready for Jesus' coming at all times. If we are not ready, we will miss his coming, and worse, we may not survive his severe judgment.[7] Those who do not choose to serve him will receive the same fate as the people of Jericho.

To reach the Promised Land (heaven), we must clear the way; that is, get rid of the enemy. Symbolically, the fall of Jericho was the coming of God's army to reclaim what is his (the earth). He already reclaimed us (the believers) when Jesus rose from the dead. However, Jesus made it clear that our task is quite different than the order to take Jericho. He has taught us a new way, one that is more difficult because it is so contrary to our natural inclination. Our fight is not to kill our fellow human beings. Rather, we are called to offer love, joy, peace, patience, kindness, goodness, faithfulness, gentleness, and self-control; against such things there is no one who can stand.[8] We are to act this way even when we are not treated with the same consideration; that is why our fight is so demanding. Nevertheless, each time we live his way, we are advancing God's cause. As Jesus taught us to pray, God wants his "will to be done on earth as it is in heaven."[9]

Be like Rahab and choose to serve God. Then, when Jesus comes, we will hear him say, "Well done, my good and faithful servant, you were faithful with little; I will put you in charge of many things; enter the joy of your master."[10]

For Further Discussion
- What would you do if you realized an angel of God came to visit you? Do you believe angels still visit the earth?
- How scared would you have been if an enemy came around your city walls six days in a row and did nothing but blow their trumpets? Then, imagine on the seventh day that the army circled the city seven times. What would you have thought?
- How much do you let your friends help you decide what is right and wrong? God has called us to seek wise counsel, so make sure your friends

and those you listen to are tuned into God's ways and *not* the ways of this world.

- Will you be ready when Jesus comes back to reclaim the earth? Will you be there to join his army? If so, how can you change how you treat your friends now? Your neighbors? Even your enemies?

For Further Study

1. 2 Kings 6:14–18—The Syrian army surrounded the walled city ready to attack, but Elisha was not concerned because there were horses with chariots of fire all around him. Elisha called on the angels to strike the enemy with blindness.

2. Daniel 10:10–14, 21—Michael, an archangel and the prince of Israel, came to the rescue of the messenger of God. Michael was assigned by God to be the prince, or protector, of Israel.

3. Revelation 5:1; 6:1–4; 8:1–7—Seven seals were opened to pronounce judgment on the earth, and when the seventh seal was opened, it revealed seven trumpets of judgment.

4. Revelation 16:16—The armies gathered at Armageddon.

5. 1 Thessalonians 4:16—Jesus will come with the voice of the archangel and the trumpet of God.

6. Revelation 19:11-21—Jesus comes and is cheered on by an army of angels, as well as by saints (believers/bondservants). He is the One called Faithful and True and the King of Kings.

7. Matthew 25:44–46—Those who did not help others as God asked were told, "To the extent you did not help others, you have not helped me. So, enter the place of eternal punishment."

8. Galatians 5:22–23—The fruit of the Spirit is love, joy, peace, patience, kindness, goodness, faithfulness, gentleness, and self-control; against such things there is no law.

9. Matthew 6:10—Jesus, in his instructions during his Sermon on the Mount, calls for us to pray for God's will to be done on earth as it is in heaven.

10. Matthew 25:21—Well done, my good and faithful servant; you were faithful with a little, so I will put you in charge of many things. Enter the joy of your master.

Chapter 3

JOSHUA CONTINUES TO LEAD ISRAEL IN BATTLE THROUGH THE PROMISED LAND

Joshua 7–12

After the victory at Jericho, the people clearly understood that God was with them. They were finally entering the Promised Land, and this time they believed it was theirs for the taking. Israel's entrance was exciting but at the same time scary, even sobering. The years of waiting would finally be worthwhile. The Israelites were entering a land God promised would be flowing with milk and honey, and he would be there to lead them in victory. So, the Lord was with Joshua, and his fame was in all the land.

Failure Is Not an Option—Or Is It?

The Israelites were now ready to attack the next city as they moved into the Promised Land. Once again, Joshua sent spies out, and the men returned saying the city of Ai was not nearly as strong as Jericho. They suggested that Joshua needed only two or three thousand people  to conquer Ai. Joshua agreed; however, as the men attacked the city, something very unexpected happened. The men of Ai were so scared that they attacked with all their might and won the battle against the Israelites.

Where was God? Why didn't he protect his family? Joshua fell on his face before God and tore his clothes as a symbol of his despair over the loss. He asked God what would happen when their enemies learned that the people of Israel had run in fear from the men of Ai. The Lord commanded Joshua,

Rise up! Why have you fallen on your face? Israel has sinned against me. During the battle of Jericho, someone took precious jewels from the people of Jericho and hid it for themselves. Therefore, I will not be with you anymore unless you recover what was taken.

The next day, Joshua gathered the people to explain the situation. He commanded the people to come before him, tribe by tribe, and as they came, God pointed out the tribe that committed the sin. Then each family within that tribe came before Joshua, and once again, God chose the family that had been disobedient. When the family presented themselves before Joshua, God pointed out Achan, the man who sinned against him and the nation of Israel.

This is a clear example of God's omniscience; he knows all. Joshua demanded that Achan tell him what he had done and give glory and praise to God. Achan responded, "I have sinned against the God of Israel. When I saw the beautiful things, I could not resist and took them for myself." If Israel was to be successful in taking over the Promised Land, the people could not have anyone among

them who was not willing to be completely obedient to God. Joshua and the people followed God's instructions to carry out a death sentence for Achan and all of his family.

Understanding Punishment

This certainly sounds like a very harsh punishment for Achan and his family. He fell into sin when he saw such beautiful things, but then he was willing to admit his sin. So, why did God order that he be killed? To understand the severe punishment, we must recognize that the Israelites were in a battle for their lives against a very strong enemy. As we learned in chapter 1 of this volume, the battle was not against just their human foes, but against spiritual forces in heavenly places who were being led by the devil. Everyone—and God meant everyone— had to be as one and be treated as one. And if God was going to perform miracles as he had done at Jericho, the whole nation had to follow *all* of his instructions.

God had been clear to Joshua and the people: nothing was to be taken for themselves in this particular battle. This was a test, and God needed to make sure his people were on board with his plans. And if each person was not willing to follow every single instruction, they would not be successful. If God let this one instance with this one family go, it would happen again, and the people would not be able to take over the land he had promised to them. This punishment certainly got their attention.

Why didn't God tell Joshua ahead of time that someone sinned? Why hadn't Joshua asked God in the same way he always had before? Maybe God needed the people to see what would happen when they were disobedient. After all, they were facing a difficult and serious task. Once the sin was purged and the man who had been disobedient was punished, God was ready once again to protect his family and lead them into the Promised Land.

We see this kind of communal punishment today. Can you remember a time when your brother or sister did not do as your parents asked, and as a result, the whole family was punished by not being able to go somewhere as planned? During my school days, my teachers would not let us go to recess until everyone was quiet. Therefore, once the teacher said be quiet, classmates began telling others who were talking to hush. I also recall a number of times when we were not allowed to go to recess because someone had been particularly rambunctious that morning. The teacher was trying to teach a valuable lesson; we were a team, and even if only one of us misbehaved, the entire class would miss out.

At first, this does not seem fair. But ask anyone who's been to military boot camp if his sergeant did not drill this concept into everyone's head. Soldiers are taught that they must follow *all* instructions, to avoid putting the entire platoon in harm's way. While we do not often deal with life-and-death situations like this, we face many instances where we must all work together as a team. And when we do not function as a cohesive team, failure will result.

It is the same with God's family. We must all work together or else our enemy, the devil, will be able to harm us. While it may seem unfair or harsh for the innocent to be punished along with the person who did the wrong, it is for the good of all to realize how important it is to work together.[2] We cannot see what God sees, so we must learn to trust him—even when we do not understand.[3] While Achan and his family lost their lives, this does not mean they weren't part of God's family; Achan repented, and I believe we will see him in heaven.

Israel Gets Back on Track

God told Joshua he would take advantage of their mistake. He gave instructions for the soldiers to pretend they were once again scared and run from the battle. And when the enemy soldiers chased them as they had before, Joshua was to have a second army in hiding to ambush the enemy when they passed by. Then, while all the soldiers of Ai were fighting the Israelites, a third army would enter the city to completely destroy the homes and all the people who remained in it. Once again, not even one person was to be left alive. As we learned earlier, it was very important to God that they *all* of his follow his instructions.

Again, this order may seem very harsh. But God was doing everything he could to give the nation of Israel the opportunity to serve him and him only; they would then receive the many blessings in store for them. If God let the inhabitants of the Promised Land remain, they would continue to serve their gods and influence the Chosen Family to follow their ways, which were evil before the Lord. I believe God was giving mankind (not just the Israelites) every chance to follow his commandments and love him the way they promised they would.

As we continue to tell the stories of this Chosen Family, we will learn that even the nation of Israel could not remain obedient to or consistently follow God's commandments. Once this was proven beyond a shadow of a doubt, God was ready to send his Son, Jesus, to show us the right way. God hoped mankind would finally accept that we need Jesus and that no one can succeed without him. By believing and trusting in Jesus, we can be brought back into the family, in spite of our weaknesses and sins.[4]

At Ai, the Israelites got the message. They were willing to follow God and the instructions he gave to Joshua, and for the most part, they did so for the rest of Joshua's life. This time, God allowed the people to keep the treasures (gold, jewels, and fine clothing) that were the spoils of victory. When we are obedient, God is ready to give and give abundantly,[5] but he needs to know we can handle it.

After the victory at Ai, Joshua built an altar where the people could worship and give sacrifices to the Lord. Joshua wrote the Ten Commandments on this altar of stones as a reminder to follow God. Do you remember my recommendation in the first story of Joshua? We should build memories of times when we know God was with us and place them in the treasure box of our heart. Even write them down so that you can read them during a time when you face difficulties; these memories can help you make it through.

Learning to Keep God in the Loop

However, just because we are willing to follow God's commandments does not mean we will not make mistakes. Even Joshua was fooled by the Gibeonites, one of the tribes of Canaan. The Gibeonites saw what happened at Jericho and Ai, and they were frightened. They devised a plan to save themselves. They dressed up in old clothes and placed old, crusty food in their backpacks. They came before Joshua and the other leaders and said they lived in a neighboring country and had traveled many days to make peace. The Israelites were fooled by their appearance and failed to inquire of God as to what they should do. Unfortunately, Israel made peace with these people and promised that they would not destroy them. But, as you may recall, God had given very clear instructions: the Israelites were not to make peace with anyone who lived in the Promised Land.

Soon, it was learned that these people had completely deceived the Chosen Family. However, God would not allow the Israelites to go back on their agreement to live in peace with this tribe. Since they could not kill them, these Gibeonites became servants of Israel.

When the neighboring kings heard about the peace treaty, they were upset with the Gibeonites for not joining them in the quest to fight against their common enemy, the Israelites. Five kings from surrounding areas gathered their armies together and prepared to destroy their neighbors. The Gibeonites sent word to Joshua for help. To keep from making another mistake, Joshua inquired of the Lord to see what he should do. God told Joshua he would be with him and Israel would be victorious.

Joshua decided to march all night to surprise and confuse the enemy. As the Israelites approached their camp, the enemy soldiers were not prepared to fight and began to run. As they fled, the Lord threw down large hail stones from heaven. More of the enemy's soldiers died from the hail than were killed by the sword. As the battle raged on, Joshua knew that once it was dark, the enemy would be able to escape, so he called on God for a mighty miracle. In the sight of his army he shouted,

O, sun, stand still at Gibeon.

God honored his request and night never came; the sun stood still, and the moon stopped. That is, the sun did not go down for a whole day. The Bible says there was no day like this ever before or after. This gave Joshua and his army the time necessary to completely destroy the enemy.

The five kings who orchestrated the attack on the Gibeonites escaped, and Joshua found them hiding in a cave. He ordered his men to roll large stones over the entrance and continue fighting the remaining soldiers. Once the battle was finished, Joshua ordered the stones to be removed. He brought the kings before Israel and declared to his leaders, "Be strong and courageous, for thus the Lord will do to all of your enemies with whom you fight."

As evening fell on the second day, Joshua hung the five kings on trees and at sunset threw them into the same cave where they were found hiding and covered the entrance with large stones. This cave became a memorial and a reminder of what God would do to the enemies of Israel. This memorial is another reminder that God wants us to recall the times he intervened in our lives so that our faith and belief in him can remain strong.

Trying to Understand the Sovereignty of God

As I shared in the first two stories of this Volume, it may be hard for us to understand why a loving God would order every one of these people to be killed. Didn't he love them? Yes, he did. So how did God show his love to the other nations and families? We are told in the Book of Romans that God's invisible and true nature is available and recognizable to anyone who truly seeks him;[6] It was the people's choice not to love him. God's plan was not to destroy mankind, but to save him. As I have described several times in this and earlier stories, God gave men and women every chance to love him, but each time, they chose not to. God first illustrated this plan in the story of Abraham (in Genesis).when God decided the only way for mankind to recognize him as the one true God was to concentrate his efforts on this one family.

To save mankind (meaning all of us), God knew that he needed this one family, and later this one nation (the Israelites), to acknowledge him as the one and only true God. And while it would take many years and many failures, the Israelites would finally accomplish this goal. Once they did, the timing was right for Jesus to come and save everyone. Now, all nations (meaning everyone) are given the opportunity to become members of God's family. Until Jesus returns to take us to heaven, our task is to recognize the sovereignty of God and accept that he is in control.[7]

Are you willing to join God's family? You can join simply by choosing to believe and trust in Jesus, the Son of God. God sent Jesus to die and rise again to save us from the punishment we would otherwise receive and deliver us into an eternal life full of blessings.

For Further Discussion

- Have you ever made a decision and soon after learned it was a big mistake? Did you realize that if you had just asked a parent, your boss, or your pastor, this person could have helped you and you could have avoided the mistake?
- Do you struggle with understanding why God commanded the Israelites to kill everyone, including women and children who were not in the battle? Did this story help you understand? If not, why do you think it was God's plan to kill those we see as innocent when Jesus clearly told us to love even our enemies?
- Joshua failed to ask God whether the Gibeonites were being honest. Are you forgetting to ask God about things in your life? He will answer you if you will listen—although it may take a while and you may have to be patient.
- God is ruler over all. Are you ready to let him to be in control? What will it benefit you to allow God to be in control of your life?

For Further Study

1. 1 Kings 16:34—Hiel the Bethelite built Jericho; he laid its foundations with the loss of Abiram, his firstborn, and set up its gates with the loss of his youngest son, Segub, according to the word of the Lord, which he spoke by Joshua, the son of Nun.

2. Ecclesiastes 4:9–12—Two are better than one because if either of them falls, the one will lift up his companion. But woe to the one who falls when there is not another to lift him up. Furthermore, if two people lie down together they keep warm, but how can one be warm alone? And if one can overpower him who is alone, two can resist him. A cord of three strands is not quickly torn apart.

3. Proverbs 3:5–6—Trust in the Lord with all of your heart; lean not on your own understanding, but acknowledge him in all of your ways, and he will make your paths straight.

4. 1 John 1:7–9—If we walk in the light as Jesus is in the light, we have fellowship with one another, and the blood of Jesus cleanses us from all sin. If we say that we have no sin, we are deceiving ourselves and

the truth is not in us. If we confess our sins, he is faithful and righteous to forgive our sins and cleanse us from all unrighteousness.

5. Luke 6:38—Give and it will be given to you, overflowing, running over; you will receive based on what you give.

6. Romans 1:18–20—For the wrath of God is revealed from heaven against all ungodliness and unrighteousness of men who suppress the truth in unrighteousness, because that which is known about God is evident within them; for God made it evident to them. For since the creation of the world, his invisible attributes, his eternal power, and divine nature have been clearly seen, being understood through what has been made so that they are without excuse.

7. God is sovereign and in control:

   a. 2 Chronicles 20:6—O Lord, the God of our fathers, are you not God in the heavens? And are you not ruler over all the kingdoms of the nations? Power and might are in your hand so that no one can stand against you.

   b. Romans 9:15–20—God said to Moses, "I will have mercy on whom I have mercy, and I will have compassion on whom I have compassion." The Scripture says regarding Pharaoh, "For this very purpose I raised you up, to demonstrate my power in you and that my name might be proclaimed throughout the whole earth." So then, he has mercy on whom he desires, and he hardens whom he desires. You will say to me then, "Why does he still find fault? For who resists his will?" On the contrary, who are you, O, man, who answers back to God? The thing molded will not say to the molder, "Why did you make me like this," will it?

Chapter 4

JOSHUA CONQUERS THE LAND AND DIVIDES IT AMONG THE TRIBES OF ISRAEL

Joshua 11–24

Joshua systematically conquered the cities and various kings who lived in the Promised Land. The enemies of Israel were known by different names, but the Bible often refers to them collectively as "Canaanites." The Israelites took them all in battle and won because Joshua and the people followed the commandments of the Lord. The Scriptures say, "The Lord hardened the hearts of the Canaanites." I interpret this to mean that these Canaanites were so intent on their own ways that when God presented them with a chance to do right, they chose to be disobedient; thus, their hearts were hardened toward God. As a result, each tribe was completely destroyed, with no survivors. Even the family of giants who scared ten of the twelve spies forty years earlier were defeated. The Israelites became rich as they divided the spoils of their conquered foes.

Dividing the Promised Land among the Chosen Family Members

While much land still remained to be conquered, the main strongholds were destroyed by Joshua and his army. God told Joshua that it was time to divide the land and let each tribe take over their own individual territory. The tribes of Reuben, Gad, and half of Manasseh were given the land east of the Jordan River. This land had been conquered under the leadership of Moses before the Israelites crossed the River. It was now time for these tribes to return home. To divide the land west of the River, Joshua, Eleazar the priest, and the heads of the households from each of the remaining ten tribes gathered to apportion the land to each family.

The tribe of Judah was allowed to choose their land first to honor the promise God gave Caleb. Caleb was the spy who, with Joshua forty years earlier, said the land could be conquered because God would be with them. Therefore, God gave

Caleb the first choice of any land within the territory of Judah.[1] He chose the land now known as Hebron to be his home. Even though Caleb was much older, he was still as strong as he was in the day Moses sent him to spy. He was ready to conquer and destroy those living in the land of Hebron. Caleb promised to give Achsah, his daughter, in marriage to the person who helped the most in conquering his land. This valiant warrior would not only marry Achsah, but he would also receive the inheritance that went with her. Othniel, who later became the first judge of Israel, captured one of the main cities and soon after married Achsah.

The land was divided among the people just as God had instructed Moses years earlier. Each family from the sons of Jacob, now referred to as the twelve tribes of Israel, received their territory. Remember, Israel was the new name God gave Jacob. Because Joseph was the favorite son of Jacob, his family was given a double blessing; therefore, two tribes are named after Joseph's sons, Ephraim and Manasseh, rather than one tribe of Joseph. If you recall, Jacob said Simeon's family would not be given a special territory because of Simeon's evil ways, so his family was given land within the tribe of Judah. Do you remember the other son of Jacob whose tribe was not given a specific territory of their own? I will remind you of this family and explain where they lived a little later.

When a family complained that the enemy seemed too strong for them, Joshua reminded them that they would be able to capture the land no matter how strong the enemy might be because God was with them. Even so, some families delayed. Joshua asked, "How long will you put off taking possession of the land, which the Lord has given you?"

I believe we have similar problems today. Do you delay because you are afraid of something you know you need to do? Even though your co-workers, parents, or friends tell you not to worry, it is very natural to give in to anxiety and procrastinate out of fear. But we need to know we can rely on God to be there with us. So, take courage and do those things you know you need to do.

To help the tribes, Joshua recommended that they send spies to survey the land and write descriptions so everybody would know the exact boundaries for their tribe. Once the land was surveyed, Joshua made a permanent record of each tribe's territory, and it was theirs forever.

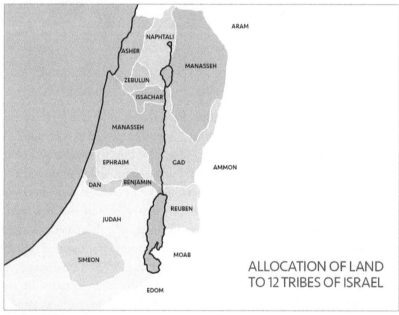

ALLOCATION OF LAND
TO 12 TRIBES OF ISRAEL

Year of Jubilee

How did God provide for each tribe to retain their land forever? In the Law of Moses, God laid out specific instructions. Not only did each tribe receive a specific territory, but also each family was given a portion of land as its own. They farmed the land for six years, but in the seventh year, they were not to farm at all. God was teaching them that the land needed to rest so it could regenerate itself; they did not have fertilizers like we do today. God promised he would provide them food in the year the land lay barren.

Then after the forty–ninth year (seven times seven) or in the fiftieth year, there would be a celebration called the Year of Jubilee. If a family sold or lost their land for any reason, they got it back during the Year of Jubilee. For example, if a family became poor and the land was taken from them, they knew it would come back to them during the jubilee celebration. To determine how much to pay for the property, the buyer had to know how many years remained until the Year of Jubilee. If the Year of Jubilee had just passed, the buyer would retain the land for forty-eight more years. On the other hand, if the Year of Jubilee was five years away, the buyer only paid to use the land for five years. In this way, God ensured everyone would keep the land within their family for generations to come. God wanted every family to have the ability to take care of themselves.[2]

This is evidence of how much God cares for each and every one of us; he will truly meet our needs. The Jewish people no longer follow these rules, and the timing for the Year of Jubilee has been lost. However, God knows the time, and I believe this celebration of Jubilee has much meaning for us today and will one day become relevant again. Just as the Israelites knew that their land would be returned one day, so this earth will be returned to God's family in the *final* great Year of Jubilee.

Let me explain. While Jesus told us that we do not know the day or hour God will send Jesus back to reclaim this world and all the saints,[3] I believe he will return during a Year of Jubilee. We just do not know which one. Satan will be required to give his rule of this world back to God; his time will have ended.[4] And while Satan will not give up his control willingly, Jesus will come and take what is rightfully his.[5] As I have explained in earlier stories, each celebration and event God gave his people in the Law of Moses is a picture foretelling some future event in God's plan for mankind. The Year of Jubilee is no different. But, as always, God will not intervene before the time is right. So, until then, Satan will continue to rule our world.

As God tells us in the New Testament, our citizenship is in heaven,[6] not here in Satan's world. Accordingly, we are to abide by God's rules and God's laws and, to the best of our ability, bring God's will on earth as it is in heaven.[7] One day Jesus will come to take the earth back from Satan.[8] And after this has been accomplished, God will create a new heaven and a new earth,[9] one free from all the devastating changes that have resulted from God's judgments. These trans-formations began with the destruction of the Garden of Eden when man (Adam) sinned and include the time God sent rain for the first time and destroyed the world with the Flood. Until Jesus returns, we are called to be on alert[10] and ready to reign with him.[11]

Levites Are Given Cities

I reminded you earlier that another of Jacob's sons was not given any specific territory for his tribe. In one of the earlier stories of Moses from Volume 1, we discussed the tribe of Levi. This family was given the responsibility of being the priests, music directors, singers, musicians, and administrators, carrying out all functions necessary to perform sacrifices, offerings, and religious duties under the Law of Moses—much like our pastors and church staff today. The Levites were given cities within each tribe's territory because God wanted each tribe to have a place to worship with access to priests for confession and making requests to God. The Levites were paid by the families of the territory in which they lived. Aaron's sons were the priests for the tribes of Judah, Simeon, and Benjamin and were given thirteen cities and pasture lands to live in and raise sheep. Other sons of Levi were priests in the other territories.

Six cities were designated as Cities of Refuge. These cities were set up to be a safe haven for anyone who killed another person. The person could escape to the designated city, and no one would be allowed to harm him until his case was heard before the elders (judges). If the elders concluded the person was killed unintentionally, without premeditation or malice, the killer's life was spared, but he had to remain in the City of Refuge until the high priest died.[12] In this way,

God was providing a way for "cooler heads to prevail." We can learn a valuable lesson from this message.

It Is Important to End Well

Joshua helped the people conquer the lands, but it was their individual responsibility to finish what the Israelites began together. And the Lord gave them rest on every side, according to all he had promised their fathers. Not one enemy was able to stand. What a powerful testimony to the nation of Israel and to us as well.

We, too, have the opportunity to give such a witness, showing through our actions that God will never fail us. We may stumble and fall, but he will be there to pick us up. I also believe God expected the Israelites to accept his gift of this Promised Land with great humility, fully understanding that it was given at a great cost that included the lives of the many men, women, and children who previously inhabited the land. And too, God expects us to accept the many wonderful blessings he provides with the same humility.

Joshua summed it all up in his farewell address to the people:

Choose for yourself today and decide whether to serve the gods of the Amorites and the Canaanites, in whose land you live, or the false gods your fathers chose to serve so often. But as for me and my house, we will serve the Lord.

We, too, have the choice to be obedient or disobedient. If we choose to be disobedient, we will pay the consequences; however, God in his mercy will be ready to forgive. Just as we will see time and time again in the stories that follow, God was always forgiving and willing to take the Israelites back, and he will do the same for us. It is our choice to either follow his commandments or follow our own ways. Once we learn that our ways are the wrong ways, God is waiting with open arms for us to return. How can we avoid wrong choices and thereby the suffering and troubles that come with them? Let's choose as Joshua did so many years ago:

"As for me and my house, we will serve the Lord."

For Further Discussion
- Can you recall a time where God delivered what he promised? God made many promises to believers. Where do you go to find these promises?
- Why is our citizenship in heaven when we live here on earth? As you think about this, remember that Satan is the ruler of this world. When does someone get their heavenly citizenship?
- Joshua chose to serve the Lord. Who will you choose?

For Further Study
1. Deuteronomy 1:35–36—Caleb was given his choice of land because of his trust in God. Only he and Joshua sided with Moses and Aaron to enter the Promised Land forty years earlier.
2. Leviticus 25:8–17—Every fiftieth year was the Year of Jubilee in which land was returned to its original owner. If the land transferred hands, the selling price was determined by the number of years before the next Jubilee.
3. Matthew 24:36—No one but the Father knows the day or hour that the Son of Man (Jesus) will return.
4. Revelation 20:1–3, 10—Satan's time on the earth ends as he is thrown into the abyss for one thousand years; afterwards, he is released for a

short time and then thrown into the lake of fire where he will be tormented day and night.

5. Revelation 19:11–13; 19–21—Jesus comes back on his white horse and wins the battle of Armageddon.

6. Philippians 3:20—Our citizenship is in heaven.

7. Matthew 6:10—The Lord's Prayer has us pray for God's kingdom to come and his will to be done on earth as it is in heaven.

8. Revelation 19:11, 14, 19–21—Jesus returns on a white horse, ready to defeat the devil and his forces.

9. Revelation 21:1–2—A new heaven and a new earth are created as the first heaven and earth have passed away, with the holy city of Jerusalem as its center.

10. Matthew 24:36, 42—No one knows the day or the hour Jesus will return. Therefore, be on the alert.

11. 2 Timothy 2:11–12—If we die with [Jesus], we will also live with him and reign with him.

12. Numbers 35:9–35—God established a City of Refuge to maintain order in the lives of his people. Instructions were provided for the trial of a person who killed another person and for the related punishment.

Chapter 5

THE PERIOD OF THE JUDGES

Judges 1–3, 9–12

Now that the Chosen Family was firmly established in the Promised Land, Joshua commissioned each tribe to take over their assigned territory. While Joshua had led the army against the strongest inhabitants of the land, there were many smaller strongholds remaining for each of the tribes to conquer on their own. He instructed them to serve the Lord so that God would continue to take care of them. Unfortunately, the tribes did not follow Joshua's instructions completely. They went to their assigned territory, but some families made peace with the existing inhabitants and lived in harmony together. While this may sound like the very thing to do, God knew the Israelites would choose to follow the ways of these new neighbors instead of the Law of Moses. It would not be long before the Israelites would learn why God asked them to wipe out their enemy instead of making peace.

The Israelites Fall Away from God's Plan

The Canaanites worshipped false gods, and each group served a different god under the rule of their own king. The religious ceremonies of the Canaanites included acts of worship that were abhorrent to God, and many times, the worship services involved evil pleasures, including immoral acts. It became very difficult for the Israelites to abstain from these evil acts because they were tempted by the pleasure such acts provided.

The Israelites soon developed a pattern of behavior that they were not able to break for almost one thousand years. They continued to call God their God, but they also joined their neighbors in their immoral religious ceremonies. From God's perspective, it was as if the Israelites were not worshipping him at all because their behavior was in complete violation of the laws he had given Moses.

God knew his people would follow their neighbors' evil ways, which explains why he instructed them to completely annihilate the Canaanites.

Is there something in your life that is so much fun that you do it even though you know it is wrong? Maybe you like being mean to your little sister or brother, or perhaps you talk about people at work behind their back. Do you say to yourself, "Sunday is the one time I get to rest or sleep in"? Maybe you go to football games or travel ball over the weekend instead of attending church. Once in while is understandable, but allowing our circumstances to eliminate or overshadow church or our time with God should not become routine. Often, God is left out when something or someone else takes his place. We must not allow this to happen.

It was not long before the Canaanites took back their lands and oppressed God's people. This action illustrates a second part of their pattern of behavior: once the oppression became too burdensome, the Israelites would cry out to God for help. God, in his mercy, would send help by raising up a leader among them who would take charge and deliver the Israelites from their enemies. These leaders were not only military commanders but also chiefs, called judges, who settled disputes among tribes and family members.

The remainder of this chapter contains stories that illustrate this pattern of indulging in sin and then crying out for deliverance.

God Calls Judges to Deliver the Chosen Family

The first time his Chosen Family cried out, God sent an angel with the following message to forewarn the people:

> *I brought you out of Egypt, and we made a covenant together. I promised to protect you. You promised not to become friends with the inhabitants of this land. You did not obey me. Therefore, I will not drive out the people so that they shall become as thorns in your side and their god shall be a snare to you.*

The anger of the Lord burned against Israel, and he gave them into the hands of their enemies. After several years, the Chosen Family realized their sin and cried out to God for forgiveness. God was moved to pity by their groaning over the oppression and affliction of the enemy, so he raised up Othniel as a judge to deliver the people. You may recall from chapter 4 that Othniel was victorious over the people of Hebron for Caleb's tribe, thereby winning Caleb's daughter Achsah for his wife. Now, Othniel went out against his enemies, and the Spirit of the Lord came mightily upon him so that he was able to prevail over his enemy

and become the first judge of Israel. Under Othniel's leadership, the people chose to follow God's commandments and had rest for the forty years Othniel was their judge.

After Othniel's death, the sons of Israel again did evil in the sight of God. So, once again, God allowed their enemies to rise up against them and possess their land. Accordingly, the Israelites served the king of Moab for eighteen years. And, once again, they cried to God for a deliverer. This time, God sent Ehud, a left-handed Benjamite, to fight against the king of Moab and his army. Ehud went before the king pretending to be subservient to him by bringing a tribute (a payment to keep the king from harming the people).

As it happened, the king of Moab was a very fat man. Ehud approached the king and said, "I have a secret message for you, O, king." As the king arose from his seat, Ehud stretched out his left hand, took the sword from his right thigh, and pressed it into the king's very fat belly. The blade and the handle went so deep that Ehud's hand sunk into his belly and was completely enclosed. Ehud left his sword in the king's belly and walked out, locking the door behind him. When the servants came to check on the king, they thought he had locked the door to go to the bathroom, so they went away. By the time the servants returned and found the king dead, Ehud was long gone.

When the Israelites learned what Ehud accomplished, they were happy to respond to his trumpet. Ehud called the troops together for battle, and the army of Moab was completely destroyed under his leadership. The land of Israel had peace for eighty years.

The Pattern of Poor Behavior Continues

Later on, after Gideon (a judge you will learn about in chapter 7) died, the sons of Israel once again turned away from God and did evil in his sight. Abimelech, Gideon's illegitimate son, decided to become the leader of the Israelites. He killed seventy of his half-brothers to clear the way and took control with the help of his mother's family. Not long afterwards, God sent an evil spirit to divide Abimelech and his mother's relatives, resulting in a civil war. Just when it seemed Abimelech would be victorious, a woman threw a large stone from a tower, crushing Abimelech's head.

After Abimelech's death, God raised another judge, Tola, to save Israel, and the people turned from their evil ways. Unfortunately, this did not last long. As soon as Tola and Jair (another judge after Tola) died, the people once again returned to their evil ways. This time, God gave them into the hands of the Philistines. After seeing the error of their ways, the people once again cried out to God,

We have sinned against you; for indeed, we have forsaken you and served other gods.

Still frustrated with the people, God lashed out,

I have saved you too many times; you have continued to forsake me and serve other gods; therefore, I will deliver you no more. Cry out to the gods which you have chosen and let them deliver you in your time of distress.

However, when the people of God *finally* put away their idols and showed God that they truly wanted to serve him, he could bear their misery no longer. So, God raised Jephthah to deliver his people. Jephthah was strong and courageous, a valiant warrior. Yet, the people were not very happy with Jephthah because he was the son of a harlot (a woman paid for her sexual favors). Despite their reluctance, with the enemy at their front door, they called on Jephthah to be their chief and lead them in their fight.

The Ammonites claimed that Israel had taken over their land. Therefore, Jephthah sent a message to their enemy, the Ammonites saying, "Israel did not take away the land of Moab, nor the land of Ammon." If you recall, Moab and Ammon were sons of Lot, and God gave this land to Lot and his descendants.[1] Jephthah further told them,

You are now trying to possess the land that we took from the Amorites (another neighboring enemy); this is not that which God gave to you. Therefore, you are doing wrong by trying to make war with us. The Lord will demonstrate who is right and will judge between the two of us by giving us victory.

But the king of Ammon disregarded the message of Jephthah, and the battle began.

Now the Spirit of God came mightily upon Jephthah, and he made a vow to the Lord: "The first person who meets me when I return in peace shall be the Lord's." Israel won the victory handily, and when Jephthah came home after the victory, his daughter was the first to come out to meet him. She was his one and only child, and she came with tambourines and dancing. When he saw her, he cried out in anguish. To honor her father, his daughter willingly became an offering to the Lord by not marrying a man; she dedicated her life to God. Each year the daughters of Israel commemorated her commitment to God to honor her. However, Jephthah did little to turn the people back to God, and he only lived six more years.

These examples demonstrate that too often during the four hundred years spent under the judges' rule, God's people served their own selfish needs, with too little attention to God.

The Difficulty in Obeying God

Why was it so hard for the nation of Israel to continually honor God and be obedient to his commandments? After all, everything seemed to go so well when they followed God: the crops grew in abundance, their families were happy, enemies stayed away from their land, and fights among the brethren were small and easily resolved.[2] But because we humans are so selfish, they continued to choose their own ways. Do you think we would have done any better?

It's easy to see what others should do and criticize their choices, but it's not so easy when we are the ones tempted to join our neighbors in selfish pleasures. Even Paul, who wrote many of the New Testament books, struggled mightily to do what was right. Even though he loved and served God as well as anyone ever has, he admitted that he often made mistakes. But, he gave credit to Jesus for helping and saving him when he did wrong.[3]

Like the Israelites, we tend to be concerned only for the moment, with no consideration of the consequences our actions will have. It is only later, after we get into trouble or learn the consequences of our mistakes, that we are sorry. Too often, we are only sorry that we got caught in our sin or have to pay the difficult price. How can we begin to let God help? Only when we are sorry for our actions with a commitment not to do it again are we truly repentant. It is then that God intervenes and comes to our rescue.

Our task is to focus on God, and when we do, we will have the wisdom and strength to see and do what is best. It is then that we can anticipate the consequences and avoid temptation—even when it is something we really want in the moment. God knows what is best for us. When we learn to trust him, we will serve him, and he will give us blessings beyond what we can imagine.[4] We do not always know when these blessings will come (in this world or in the next), but the Bible is clear that the more we sacrifice, the more blessings we will receive in eternity.[5]

For Further Discussion
- Can you see why it was so difficult for the Israelites to follow God's plan?
- Often a new minister will come to a church, and many good things will happen. Then, when the minister leaves, everything seems to fall apart. Do you have an explanation? How does this compare with the judges in Israel?
- What would tempt you and cause you to fall away from God's plan?

For Further Study
1. Deuteronomy 2:9, 19—God gave the land east of the Promised Land to Moab and Ammon, the sons of Lot. He instructed the Israelites to leave this land alone because it was not theirs.
2. Deuteronomy 28:1–14—God promised a great harvest, a happy family, and successful lives if his people obeyed the Law of Moses.
3. Romans 7:15–25—Paul said he struggled to do what he knew was the right thing to do; he realized that evil was in him, but he also knew to call on God, who would help him and save him from all of his sins.
4. Ephesians 3:20—Now to him who is able to do beyond all we ask or think, according to the power that works within us.
5. 1 Peter 1:6–7—Although we may suffer various tribulations in this life, those who suffer will be glorified with Jesus when he returns.

Chapter 6
DEBORAH AND BARAK
Judges 4–5

As we have seen through the previous stories about God's Chosen Family, the nation of Israel had a difficult time obeying the commandments of God. After their leader Ehud died, the Israelites once again did evil in the sight of God. And as a result, God allowed Jabin, king of the Canaanites, to take over their land; Jabin treated the Israelites very harshly. After twenty years of domination and cruelty, Israel cried out to God for help. At the time, Israel did not have a king, so God raised judges (leaders) to lead his people to victory over their enemies, provide guidance, and resolve disagreements among the people.

Deborah, a Prophetess and Judge in Israel
In this story God sent his promise of deliverance through a prophetess named Deborah. Like a male prophet, she conveyed messages from God to the people. She was also called by God to judge Israel. The Bible gives no explanation why a woman was given this leadership role, but we do know that the men were not leading the people to follow God. The sons of Israel came to her for judgment at a place known as the Palm Tree of Deborah.

However, she was not a military leader. She heard from God that Barak was the chosen military leader to deliver his people from the oppression of Jabin. Yet, Barak was not so confident; hence, he told her, "I will go only if you will go with me."

Deborah agreed but told Barak he would not get full credit for the victory. She prophesied that a woman would kill Sisera, the leader of Jabin's army. When Sisera learned that Barak was coming after him, he gathered all nine hundred of his iron chariots to frighten the army of Israel. Sisera hoped the Israelites would be too scared to fight. But Deborah, knowing that God was on the side of the Israelites, declared to Barak, "Behold, the Lord has gone out before you." With this confirmation, Barak led the charge, and as Deborah promised, the Lord helped the Israelites crush the army of Sisera and his iron chariots. However, Sisera escaped with Barak in pursuit.

A Surprise Ending to the Battle

Sisera escaped to a city where the people were not part of the fight; he found refuge with a man named Heber—or so he thought. Heber's wife, Jael, had other plans. Jael invited Sisera to hide in her house and pretended to protect him by placing a large rug over him to hide him from Barak. However, after Sisera was securely settled in his hiding place, Jael took a tent peg and a hammer and drove the peg through the rug and into his temple. When Barak arrived some time later, Jael took him inside to show him Sisera's dead body under the rug.

The first time I read the story, I certainly expected that Deborah would be the one to kill the enemy leader. Didn't you? However, Deborah was not the military leader; that was Barak's job. But because he was not willing to trust God without Deborah's assistance, God took away some of Barak's credit for the victory. This does not mean God did not use Barak in a mighty way. In the same way, just because we disappoint God does not mean he will not use us. Still, we do miss out on some of the blessings God wants to give us when we do not fully trust him.[1]

In Bible times, it was important for the leader of the army to be recognized as the victor in front of his people. To receive credit for the victory, the triumphant leader would kill the enemy's leader for all to see. However, in this case, Barak lost the privilege to kill Sisera.

As Deborah prophesied, a woman (Jael) killed Sisera, the leader of Israel's enemy. As a result, Jael became famous throughout Israel. Deborah and Barak wrote a song in her honor and gave her credit for sealing the victory over their enemy. So, Barak did not mind sharing the credit with a woman, and he gave no resistance in sharing the leadership role with Deborah for the rest of his life. For the next forty years, Deborah and Barak judged Israel in peace.

This story is one of the few places in the Old Testament where a woman was given leadership responsibilities with authority over men.[2] By now you may have discovered my pattern of interpreting these Old Testament stories; if so, you will know I believe God is trying to teach us lessons by revealing his ways through these historical events. Why did God choose to share this story with us? And why did God place Deborah in this position of authority?

Relating the Message of Deborah and Barak to Today

How does this story relate to us today? If you recall, one of the punishments given to the woman in the Garden of Eden was for man to be in "authority" as the head of the family.[3] However, what if a man needs or requests a woman's assistance, like Barak did with Deborah? Or what if a man fails to perform his duties, thus abdicating (giving up) his role? A void would be left by each man's failure. Because God's people were once again disobedient, it is possible that God anointed Deborah as judge because the men of her time failed in their responsibility.

I believe the events of this story parallel what is happening in our world today. With changes in technology and lifestyle, it is less common for women to stay home to take care of daily responsibilities. Men have needed and requested women's assistance in the workplace—similar to how Barak would only lead with Deborah's help. And too, like the Israelites, man has often not fulfilled his assigned leadership responsibilities—both as a leader in the church and as the head of his household. As a result, women have rightly (I believe) taken on leadership positions.

However, some admirable Christian churches still strongly believe it is man's sole responsibility to lead the church, and the women of those congregations may agree. Certainly, Paul felt this way when he told the Corinthians that women were to be silent in the church.[4] Is it possible that both points of view may be right?

Scripture clearly supports God's view of man and woman as equals, both at creation and for eternity.[5] So why did God put man in authority? It was Eve's choice, when she ate the forbidden fruit, that resulted in woman's assigned role.[3] If women can now be leaders, what changed? Let's examine the Scripture for insight on this shift in roles.

The Role of Women in the Church

Since the beginning of the twentieth century, disagreements about a woman's role in society and, more specifically, in the church have arisen. Today, many great female workers and leaders serve in the church. But just because women have taken on a role of leadership does not mean God endorsed it. In the past, society did not generally allow women in a position of leadership, and so it was in the church. Since society has changed, many Christian leaders now believe that allowing a woman to take on a leadership role in the church is acceptable. But just because society changed does not necessarily mean that churches should follow.

Significant evidence in the Bible limits the leadership roles women should have in the church.[6] Paul was clear when he said he did not allow women to lead in his church; he believed that this directive came from God.[7] Peter said that women were to submit or be subject to the authority of their husbands.[8] However, we have evidence that not everyone followed Paul's requirement for women to be silent in church, and some passages in Scripture support broader roles for women in the church.

First, we may have a misconception of God's role for women in Bible days. The Book of Proverbs reveals a much broader perspective of woman as a co-head of the family, with a position in society as well. Proverbs 31 describes God's view of an *ideal* wife:

An excellent wife, who can find? For her worth is far above jewels.[9]

She considers a field and buys it; from her earnings, she plants a vineyard.[10]

Did you think buying and planting were only a "man's job"? Not so, according to Proverbs. The excellent wife is also called upon to make herself strong. And not only did she make clothing, but she sold the clothes to the tradesmen in the market. These scriptures encourage women to be good business people.

Proverbs goes on to say that a woman is encouraged to share her wisdom, and it is important to listen to her teachings on kindness.[11] The description of the "excellent" wife ends by saying a woman who fears the Lord is the one who shall be praised.[12]

Did you know that Jesus' ministry was financed by women?[13] And that women were part of the group of disciples who followed him as he traveled from place to place?[14] While his twelve apostles hid or ran in fear after his arrest, a group of women were with him at the end as they watched him suffer on the cross; these women were also the ones who went to the tomb after Jesus' death and to whom Jesus first appeared after his resurrection.[15]

And, significantly, Philip, one of the seven chosen to help the twelve apostles serve widows, had four daughters who were all prophetesses,[16] which means they were not silent in church. In fact, even Paul gave instructions on the proper way for women to pray and prophesize in the church.[17] So Paul recognized that not all churches followed his practices for women to be silent.

But, for the most part, women played a supporting role. And until recently, Paul's practice of having only men in authority was the predominant view. Has God endorsed a change? I believe the story of Deborah and Barak is a prophecy that became a reality beginning in the twentieth century. As he has done many times before, God had to find another source to get his Word to mankind. If we are not following God's plan, he will give our responsibilities and blessings to someone else; as with Deborah and Jael, he has chosen women to assist as his emissaries today. The need was created when men requested assistance from women and also when men failed in their responsibility to be strong leaders. God is giving shared responsibility to men and women to lead as he did with Deborah and Barak. Jesus said, "If the people fall silent, the rocks will cry out;"[18] so why not women?

Too many men have remained silent and need assistance from their "helpmate." Does this negate the punishment God gave the woman in the Garden of Eden? Not necessarily. Otherwise, you could also say man was trying to reverse his punishment when he invented the tractor to reduce the hard labor required to farm the land. While this example may not be exactly the same, it is similar enough to make the point.

A Personal Testimony

When I was twelve, a woman led a revival in my home church. Boy, was a female preacher unusual in 1961! One night she told us that it was up to each individual to choose whether to believe that Jesus came to save us from our sins.

She asked, "Does anyone want to accept Jesus as their Savior tonight?" I grew up in the church; I knew who God was, and all along, I accepted what I was taught about Jesus. But I never, as she put it, "specifically chose to believe" that Jesus was my Lord and Savior.

So that night, I walked to the front of the church to claim Jesus as my Savior. I cannot say I was a whole lot different after that, but things in my life were changed. From that day on, I have been confident that I have a Savior who died for me, even if I fail to follow all of the commandments. I know I have a Heavenly Father and a Savior who love me and want me to be with them forever. That same year, I began to read my Bible most every day, and to this day, fifty-seven years later, I have continued this practice.

I believe very strongly that my subtle but significant change was, in part, due to God working through a woman. While our personal "experience" cannot overrule God's Word, it can help us properly interpret Scripture. I am thankful for this woman who spoke that night, and I believe she was a minister of God. Have I justified what I want to believe, or have I properly interpreted the Bible? While it was many years later before I made the connection, the story of Deborah and Barak helped me understand God's willingness for women to be active in church leadership.

Resolving Differences

As I have pointed out, even during the early years of the church, not everyone followed the same plan and role for women. Paul said women were to be silent in the church,[7] while other churches in Paul's day allowed women prophetesses.[16, 17] We are no different today. I do not believe either group is wrong as long as they are following God's lead. Paul stayed in the house with Philip whose daughters were prophetesses.[19] Clearly, even with conflicting viewpoints, these two were able to get along. What are we to conclude?

If men take full responsibility in church leadership and the church believes men should maintain this role, let's be thankful that men of God are willing to stand up and be counted as God's leaders. After all, they are following the plan laid out by Paul in the New Testament. And by the same token, I encourage those churches who do not allow women to perform certain leadership roles to be accepting of other churches who do on the basis that these women are carrying out the role requested, or filling positions vacated by men, just as Deborah and Jael did in this Old Testament story.

This is my account and my interpretation; each of us is accountable to God to search the truth the Bible has to offer. *If you seek God's wisdom and guidance with the assistance of the Holy Spirit, he will give you the proper interpretation.* We need to make sure we are not merely justifying what we want to believe. When we are *truly* seeking to properly interpret God's Word, I believe God will honor our differing opinions and conclusions if we learn how to disagree in love and with respect for one another.

For Further Discussion

- Did you learn from Barak that we need to trust God, even when are afraid? Our trust belongs in God, not in others. Isn't it nice to know that God understands and will send help for you anyway?
- What does your church say about women in positions of church leadership?
- No matter what you believe about the role of a woman in the church, do you see how we will all be equal in God's eyes in heaven?
- Because we are all different, we will not all think alike. So, we must learn to disagree in love, respecting the opinions and feelings of others. However, it is equally important to stand firm for what God says is right and wrong.

For Further Study

1. 1 Corinthians 3:15—Actions and activities in our life that are not beneficial to God will result in a loss of the blessings God has in store for us.
2. Women leaders and prophetesses in other sections of the Old Testament:
   a. 2 Kings 11:1–4—Athaliah seized the throne after her son's death and ruled over the Kingdom of Judah for seven years.
   b. 2 Kings 22:14–20—Israel's leaders went to Huldah, a prophetess, for advice.
3. Genesis 3:16—Part of Eve's punishment for eating the apple was that man (her husband) would be the one in charge.
4. 1 Corinthians 14:34–35—Women are to be silent in the church.
5. Men and women were equal at creation and will continue to be equal in eternity:
   a. Galatians 3:28
   b. 1 Corinthians 11:11–12

6. Limitations were placed on the role of women in church; however, it is not clear if there was a rule against women leaders:

   a. 1 Timothy 2:12—Paul told Timothy, regarding the role of women in the church, "I do not permit a woman to teach or to have authority over a man, but to be silent."

   b. 1 Corinthians 14:34—Paul calls for women to be silent in church.

   c. 1 Timothy 3:1–16—Paul gives Timothy instructions for leaders. When describing the top role in the church (bishop), he only lists men; when describing a supporting leadership role (deacon), people have different interpretations on whether women could take on this position.

   d. 1 Corinthians 11:5—Paul acknowledges that women are allowed to pray and prophesy, so it must have been a personal decision that he preferred women to be silent—not something that God limited.

7. 1 Corinthians 14:34–38—Paul shares that women should be silent in the church and that he received this command from God.

8. 1 Peter 3:1–2—Women should recognize the role of the husband as the one in authority.

9. Proverbs 31:10—An excellent wife is worth much more than jewels.

10. Proverbs 31:16—This excellent wife buys a field, makes a profit on it, and expands it by planting a vineyard.

11. Proverbs 31:26—A woman teaches on kindness.

12. Proverbs 31:30—A woman who fears the Lord will be praised.

13. Luke 8:3—Jesus' ministry was financed by wealthy women.

14. Luke 8:1–2—Women were among Jesus' disciples who followed him as he traveled from place to place.

15. A group of women watched as Jesus suffered on the cross and went to the tomb after his death. Jesus first appeared to these same women after his resurrection:

    a. Matthew 27:55–56

    b. John 19:25

    c. Matthew 28:1–8

16. Acts 21:9—Philip's daughters were prophetesses, which means they spoke of messages from God. (Also see Acts 6:1–5.)

17. 1 Corinthians 11:5—Paul instructs women to pray and prophesize in church with their head covered.

18. Luke 19:39–40—Jesus told the Jewish leaders that if the people became silent, the rocks would cry out.

19. Acts 21:8–9—Paul stayed at the house of Philip on his way to Jerusalem. Philip's daughters were prophetesses.

Chapter 7

GIDEON, THE LEAST BECOMES THE GREATEST

Judges 6–8

After forty years of peace, the Israelites once again did evil in the sight of God, and the Lord gave them into the hands of the Midianites for seven years. The power of the Midianites was so strong that God's People hid themselves in caves to escape their wrath. At harvest time, the Midianites would steal the produce after all the hard work was complete. Israel realized their need and again cried out to the Lord for help.

God Calls an Unlikely Leader

God sent a prophet to tell Israel of their evil ways and how disobedient they had been. At the same time, God sent an angel to Gideon, one of the sons of Manasseh. The angel introduced himself to Gideon by saying, "The Lord is with you, O, valiant warrior." Gideon was perplexed. If the Lord was with him, why were his people struggling with their enemy? Gideon felt abandoned by God, but God knew better and said to Gideon, "Go in your strength and deliver Israel from the hand of Midian."

Gideon was frightened and asked God how he could deliver Israel. Gideon explained that Manasseh was not a strong tribe and his family was not highly regarded in Manasseh; further, he was the youngest son in his family, with no position to claim any leadership or authority. Remember, the youngest son in a family inherited the least and was subject to whatever his oldest brother would give him. In that case how was God expecting Gideon to take on any leadership role? When the angel first came to him, he was making bread in a wine press to try to keep the Midianites from finding out what he was doing. He was that frightened. How could he take on the Midianites and help deliver his people?

Gideon's position within the nation of Israel gives me a chance to share an important lesson. God is not interested in our social position or status here on earth. Once again, we learn that God's ways are not like man's ways. He can and does use anyone willing to serve him—from the greatest to the least.[1] He is *not* a respecter of persons.[2] You may feel as lowly as Gideon, the youngest brother in an insignificant family, but God can and will use you. Be ready for his call, for he is prepared to give you what you need. We will see that God allowed Gideon to test him so that he could be sure it was God telling him to do this task, which he did not feel worthy of doing. God proved over and over to Gideon that he would be with him all the way. And if God calls, he will do the same for you. So, even if you do not feel you are strong enough, smart enough, or popular enough, you can trust that God will be there with you and give you what you need—supernaturally, if necessary.

Gideon Defends the Name of God

Gideon asked God, "If I have found favor, please give me a sign that it is you speaking to me." According to the angel's instructions, Gideon prepared an altar and placed the meat of a young goat and bread on it. Then the angel touched the meat and the bread with his staff, and fire sprang up from the altar and consumed the food. At once the angel of the Lord vanished from his sight. Until this point, Gideon did not understand that an angel was in his presence, but now he was afraid for his life. However, God spoke to his heart and convinced him that he would not die. Gideon then dedicated the altar to God and named it "The Lord Is Peace."

That night, God gave Gideon specific instructions to take two bulls to offer as a sacrifice. Before the sacrifice, he was told to pull down the altar of Baal and Asherah, the god and goddess of the Midianites. In their place, God wanted an altar built where the bulls could be offered as a sacrifice, using the wood of the Asherah idol. Gideon took ten men from his father's household and did as the Lord instructed. He did it by night because he was too afraid of the Midianites.

When the Midianites arose early in the morning, they discovered what had happened. "Who did this thing?" they questioned. It did not take them long to find out that it was Gideon. The men immediately went to Gideon's house and demanded that he be delivered to them. But Gideon's father said, "Will you contend for Baal? If he truly is a god, he will take revenge himself" (that is, will you do Baal's work for him?). The Midianites left without Gideon, whose name was changed that day to Jerubbaal, which means, "Let Baal contend against him."

Gideon Needs Assurances with War at Hand

The Midianites were angry and sent their army to the Valley of Jezreel to make war with the Israelites and punish them for their insolence. But Gideon now had the Spirit of the Lord with him, so he blew a trumpet calling the army of Israel to come to help. Gideon still wanted to know that God was with him, so he set up a test. He put out a fleece of wool on the threshing floor and declared, "If there is dew on the fleece only and the ground is dry, then I will know that God will deliver Israel through me." The next morning the ground was dry and the fleece was wet, so much so that there was a bowl of water drained from the fleece. But Gideon was still unsure. Therefore, he asked God again, "Do not let your anger burn against me. But may I ask one more favor? This time let the fleece be dry and let there be dew on the ground." And God did just as Gideon asked. Gideon was now ready to do battle.

Jerubbaal, as Gideon was now called, brought his army to the spring of Harod. But God was concerned that there were too many in Gideon's army. God did not want the people boasting that they were responsible for the victory. He wanted them to know it was God who delivered them. Gideon had an army of thirty-two thousand; the Midianites had an army of 135,000. It sounds to me as if Gideon did not have enough soldiers, but God thought otherwise and he instructed Gideon to tell everyone who was frightened to go home. Twenty-two thousand left camp and returned home. Now it really looked as if Gideon was at a disadvantage. But God was not finished; he felt there were still too many in Gideon's army. To go to war in those days, each army would line up at opposite ends of the valley, and up to one thousand men from each side would march to the middle. If Gideon's men won overwhelmingly each time, they may surely think *they* won the battle, rather than God.

Consequently, God instructed the remaining ten thousand men to take a drink from the spring of Harod. When the men went to drink, three hundred men knelt down and brought the water to their mouth and lapped it up, while 9,700 others put their face down in the water and drank directly from the spring.

Who do you think were the better-prepared soldiers? Of course, it was the three hundred who knelt down and brought the water to their mouth, keeping their eyes up, looking for any danger. Surprisingly, God sent the 9,700 men home. This left Gideon with only three hundred men to fight the enormous army of Midianites.

God Delivers the Victory

God told Gideon that he was now ready for battle and when the victory was won, they could not deny that it was God who delivered them. That night, God gave Gideon insight into his plan; he wanted to relieve Gideon of any remaining fear and show him that he (God) was in charge. He instructed Gideon to take his servant with him and sneak to the camp of the Midianites. When Gideon came to the campsite, a man was relating a dream to his fellow soldiers, saying, "Behold, I had a dream; a loaf of barley bread was tumbling into the camp, and it struck our tent and turned it upside down so that the tent lay flat." One of the soldiers responded, "This is nothing less than the sword of Gideon; God has given Midian into his hand."

When Gideon heard the men speaking, he bowed in worship. He returned to the camp and said to his men, "Arise, for the Lord has given the Midianites into your hands." Gideon divided the three hundred men into three companies and gave each a trumpet, an empty pitcher, and a torch. He told them to look to him and do as he instructed. Each of the three armies of one hundred men circled around the entire camp of the Midianites. At the proper time, they would all blow the trumpets, smash the pitchers, wave their torches, and proclaim, "A sword for the Lord and for Gideon." But instead of charging the camp, the three hundred men stood in place. The Midianites awoke from their sleep, crying out and scrambling in different directions in total confusion. It was still dark, and they were so scared that they picked up their swords and started killing one another, thinking each other was the enemy. Those who were not killed fled.

Now it was time to call out the Israelite reinforcements from the tribe of Ephraim to chase down the Midianite soldiers. The men of Ephraim killed Oreb and Zeeb, two of the kings of Midian. When they brought the heads of these two leaders to Gideon, they asked, "Why didn't you call us to fight against the Midianites?" They were very upset with Gideon, but he was very smooth in his reply, "What have I done that can compare with what you've accomplished by killing these two kings?" As a result, their anger subsided and the men of Ephraim were satisfied with their contribution.

Gideon, with his three hundred men and now others with him, continued to fight all day long, and at the end of the day, they became weary. He asked the men of the cities of Succoth and Penuel to provide bread and water to his men. These men were not convinced that Gideon would win the battle, so they refused his request. Gideon promised to take revenge when his victory was secure. At this time, there were only fifteen thousand men left in the Midianite army; one hundred and twenty thousand were already dead. After the remaining fifteen thousand men were captured and killed, Gideon returned to punish the men who refused to give his men bread and water.

Gideon then turned his attention to the two remaining captured kings of Midian. Because they killed members of his family, he pronounced a death sentence on these two kings. He first tried to let his son have the honor of killing them, but he was too young and was afraid to do it; so, Gideon killed them himself. While our culture today sees this as too violent, it was the way people in Old Testament times established authority and respect.

Understanding the Harsh Lifestyle of the Times

All of this beating and killing seems out of place to us. Throughout history, what is acceptable has changed. Society follows what the leaders of the day believe is right. Unfortunately, leaders seldom ask God what he thinks. Quite a number of things have changed in American culture since I was young person. I think these changes go against what God would choose, but those making decisions do not agree. And God has chosen to allow man to make the decisions. Unfortunately, but understandably, God will also let us pay the consequences for our poor decisions.

But why would God honor such violent actions? It is not that God honors the lifestyle of the times; rather, he chooses not to intervene. It is hard for us to accept, but remember, he decided many years ago that the people turned so fiercely against him that he would concentrate on just one family, the family of Abraham, Isaac, and Jacob. And Jesus told us that God will accept certain actions of man that are not part of his plan—even actions committed by those who were members of the Chosen Family[3]—as he works to accomplish his greater purpose: to reconcile mankind back to him. So, from an eternal viewpoint, God has our best interest in mind.

The men of Israel wanted Gideon to rule as king over them. But Gideon, knowing God and knowing his place, said, "I will not rule over you, nor shall my son; the Lord shall rule over you." Gideon did ask that each man give him a gold earring worn by the Midianite soldiers. Unfortunately, contrary to God's commandments, Gideon used the rings to make an idol. Nonetheless, Gideon judged Israel for forty years, and except for this indiscretion, he served God faithfully, and Israel remained at peace with their enemies.

Are you ready to follow God when he calls you to do a job that seems too big? Too many church leaders today are falling away from what is right before God. They are too interested in their own desires and have forgotten God. God is waiting for someone who will join his cause.[4] If you listen carefully, you may learn he is calling you. If you will be obedient, you will receive many blessings and see God work miracles for you, just like he did for Gideon. He may be calling you to wake up the church leaders and lead us all back to God.

For Further Discussion
- Do you ever feel unworthy? Do you ever feel you are not special? Gideon did not think he was worthy or special, but God knew otherwise. God has special plans for each of us. How can you discern his plans for you?
- Do you see how God gives assurances when we are unsure or when we step out into dangerous territory for him? He delivered miracles three different times for Gideon; God understood Gideon needed reassurance because of his insecurity and the gravity of the task.
- Why does it seem even the best people make mistakes, as Gideon did? How can you avoid the trap?

For Further Study
1. Jesus taught throughout his ministry that the least are the greatest in his kingdom. Jesus not only taught this message, he also lived it by example: (1) when he left the throne of God to become a man; (2) when he washed the disciples' dirty, filthy feet; and (3) when he died on the cross and rose to save us as the ultimate example of humility and sacrifice:
   a. Matthew 20:25–28—This world has one view of the greatest, but in God's world, the greatest is the least, the servant. Jesus did not come to be served, but to serve as a substitute for us.

b. Philippians 2:6–8—Jesus gave up his heavenly throne and humbled himself and became a man to die on the cross for us all.

c. John 13:13–15—Jesus showed the disciples that while he was their teacher, he performed the lowliest of duties, which was to wash someone's feet. He wanted them to follow his example of serving others.

d. Hebrews 7:25–27; 9:14–15, 24, 28—The perfect sacrifice of Jesus, who died on the cross to save each of us who believe.

2. James 2:1–3—God does not like it when we show favoritism. Everyone is equally special to him.

3. Matthew 19:7–8—God allowed the Israelites certain privileges (in this case, divorce) that were really not his best for man because he understood their weakness.

4. 2 Timothy 2:1–7—We are all called to join as soldiers of Christ. As any soldier, we must endure hardship; as any athlete, we must work hard at that which God has called us to do.

Chapter 8
SAMSON, JUDGE OF ISRAEL: PART 1
Judges 13–16

The Birth of Samson

In the times of the judges, before there were kings in Israel, the Philistines ruled over the Israelites because, once again, the sons of Israel were doing evil in the sight of the Lord. There was a certain man from the family of Dan named Manoah, whose wife was not able to have children. One day, the angel of the Lord appeared to Manoah's wife and told her that she would give birth to a son. Because the Lord had special plans for her son, the angel told her that she was not to drink any wine or eat any unclean food. After she gave birth to the son, she was not to ever cut his hair; he was to live his entire life as a Nazirite.

Under the Law of Moses, a Nazirite could live his life dedicated to the Lord for a week, a month, or a year, but in this very special case, her son was to live his entire life as a Nazirite. And if he followed God's instructions, he would be given special powers that God would use to help the Israelites against their enemy, the Philistines. He would become the closest thing to a superhero that this world has ever seen, and his strength would be so great that he could overcome an entire army by himself.

Manoah's wife ran to tell her husband about the visit from the "man" of God. She did not yet know the visitor was an angel. Manoah prayed and asked God to send this man to return. God listened to his request and sent the angel to visit once again. The angel gave instructions further to raise the boy in the ways of the Lord. Now, Manoah still was not convinced this was an angel, so he asked him to stay for dinner. The angel would not eat with them, but said they could make a sacrifice to the Lord. Manoah and his wife built an altar and put a lamb upon it. They set fire to the altar, and the angel of the Lord did wonders for them before he flew into the fire and vanished.

What a special blessing this was for Manoah and his wife. Still a bit frightened, they left reflecting upon this opportunity to have a special son of God. In less than a year, Manoah's wife gave birth to a son and named him Samson; as the boy grew up, the Lord blessed him.

Prior to the angel's visit, Manoah and his wife assumed God was not pleased with them because they were not able to have children. But in reality, God was waiting for just the right time to send a special blessing to this family. We do not always get what we want when we want it. So, it is okay to ask God if you are doing something wrong or if you need to change what you are doing. And if you are willing to listen closely, God will tell you what you need to do differently.[1] Or, as was the case with Manoah, you may not be doing anything wrong; you may just need to be patient and wait.[2] If we can learn to be patient and trust God, he will answer our request in *his* timing, and the wait will be more than worth it.[3]

Samson Marries a Philistine

After Samson became a man, he visited Timnah, a Philistine city, and met a beautiful woman. He told his mother and father that he wanted her to be his wife. At first, they were upset because they wanted Samson to marry a woman from their own country. However, Samson's mind was set, so his parents agreed for him to marry her. They did not realize that God was using this as an occasion for Samson to take vengeance on the Philistines. God chose a very unusual way to make this happen.

Samson was stronger than any man who ever lived on the earth, and he was given special powers to defeat Israel's enemy. God needed Samson to get angry with the Philistines so that he would use his strength against them. Up until this time, Samson had been friends with them, but God would use a disagreement to establish Samson as a judge of Israel. Remember, a judge was a person God chose to lead the Israelites in battle against their enemy and to make sure they were following the ways of God, including handling disputes among the people.

One day as he was going to visit his future wife, Samson was attacked by a lion. The spirit of God came mightily upon Samson, and he tore apart the lion with his bare hands and cast him aside. He told no one what he did. Some days later, on the way to his wedding, Samson saw that a beehive was housed in the bones of the lion he had killed.

During Bible times, a wedding lasted for seven days. On the first day, Samson was entertaining thirty friends of the bride's family. He decided to play a game with them and told them he would give each of them an expensive coat if they could solve his riddle. However, if they could not solve the riddle within the seven days, then each one would owe him a special coat. The thirty men agreed to Samson's challenge, and he told them the following riddle:

Out of the eater came something to eat; out of the strong came something sweet.

On the fourth day of the wedding celebration, the Philistine men became very concerned that they could not figure out Samson's riddle. Fearing he might win the bet, they went to Samson's wife and told her that if she did not find out the answer, they would kill her and all of her family. So, she went before Samson and pleaded with him to give her the answer. He responded that if he had not even told his own mother and father, he certainly would not tell her. But she continued to nag and plead with Samson for the answer every day. On the seventh day, he got so tired of her asking that he finally relented and told her how he killed the lion and later discovered honey inside the lion's bones. Well, of course, she went right to the family friends and told them the answer to the riddle. The thirty friends then came before Samson and boasted, "What could be sweeter than honey, and what is stronger than a lion?"

Samson Fights the Philistines

Samson immediately knew that his wife had given them the answer. He was angry with her and with her friends, so that night, he went out among the Philistines and killed thirty men. He then took their coats to the thirty wedding guests to honor his bet. This marked the beginning of a war between Samson and the Philistines.

Have you ever been so angry that you did something wrong but later felt bad about it? This is what happened to Samson. After his anger subsided, he went back to get his wife, only to find that his father-in-law had given her to another man. Samson became furious. Her father tried to appease Samson by giving him his younger daughter in marriage, but Samson wanted his wife. This time, Samson felt his anger was justified and told the Philistines that the punishment he would give out was their own fault.

He caught three hundred foxes and used the tails of two foxes to tie a fiery torch between them. It was harvest time for the grain and grapes, so Samson let the foxes out into the fields, burning the entire crop.

After the Philistines found out what Samson had done, they killed his wife and her family and set out to find Samson. But Samson found them first and single-handedly won a great battle, slaughtering many Philistines because they killed his wife and her family.

When Samson moved to a city in Judah, the Philistines gathered an army to go after him. The men of Judah (one of the twelve tribes of Israel) were scared of the Philistines and went looking for Samson. Remember, the Philistines were much stronger than the people of Israel at that time. When the men of Judah found Samson, they argued with him over the problems he was causing. Finally, Samson agreed to let them tie him up and turn him over to the Philistines. But the men of Judah had to promise they would not kill him. Samson had a plan.

They bound Samson with two brand new ropes and brought him to the Philistines. Once the men of Judah were safely gone, Samson tore the ropes off his arms as if they had been thin threads. As he broke loose from the ropes, he saw the jawbone of a donkey lying beside the road. He picked it up and started swinging it at the Philistines. He killed one thousand Philistines that day and escaped their grasp. After he escaped, Samson called to God for water as he was extremely thirsty from the battle. God honored his request and opened the earth to provide Samson water to drink.

I am convinced that God will give us special powers when we need to serve him.[4] Our power may not be quite so obvious as Samson's strength, but Jesus gave seventy of his disciples the authority to cure the sick and heal the lame.[5] Jesus later says that we will do even greater things than occurred while he was here on earth.[6] While all of God's gifts are not supernatural, each of us are given gifts to use in carrying out the service God has called us to.

We end part 1 with Samson in place as a judge in Israel, with the Philistines under control. The Philistines were more worried about how to beat Samson than oppressing the Israelites, so God's plan was working. A good lesson from this story is not to put God in a box. This was certainly not the traditional way God raised leaders to deliver his people from their enemy, but as we have learned in earlier stories, God's ways are not our ways.[7] So let's open our spiritual eyes and listen to what God has to tell us.[8] He might surprise us with something new and innovative for us to do for him. We have more to learn in part 2 of Samson's story.

For Further Discussion
- This is not the first time, and it will not be the last time, that a married couple longed for a baby. What have you learned about good people who have not been able to get something they wanted?
- How would it feel to be so strong that you could fight, defend, and even take advantage of others because of your strength? How do you think God would want you to use the special power he gave you?
- God gives us all special gifts to use to serve him. Do you know what your gift(s) is?

For Further Study
1. James 1:5—If any of you lacks wisdom, you should ask God, who gives generously to all without finding fault, and it will be given to you.
2. Psalms 37:7, 9—Rest in the Lord and wait patiently for him. Those that wait upon the Lord, they shall inherit the land.
3. Luke 1:5–8, 11, 23–24—Zacharias and Elizabeth were an older couple who were both righteous before God, but they had no children. An angel, Gabriel, came to tell Zacharias that God had answered his prayer, and soon they had a baby boy named John (later known as John the Baptist).
4. God's gift to the believers:
   a. Romans 12:6–8
   b. 1 Corinthians 12:4–11
   c. Ephesians 4:7, 11–13
5. Luke 10:1, 8–9, 17—Jesus commissioned seventy others to heal the sick, and the seventy returned from their mission praising God and saying even the demons obeyed them.
6. John 14:12—Jesus told his disciples that if they believed in him and the works (miracles) he did, then they would do even greater works because he would go to the Father and plead their case before him.
7. Isaiah 55:9—For as the heavens are higher than the earth, so are [God's] ways higher than your ways and [his] thoughts higher than your thoughts.
8. 2 Corinthians 5:7—Walk by faith, not by sight (walking by faith is walking with our spiritual eyes and not our physical eyes). Also see 2 Kings 6:15–17 where Elisha prayed for his servant's eyes to be open to see the angels and God's chariots of fire surrounding his enemy. All he could see with his physical eyes were the enemy soldiers.

Chapter 9
SAMSON, JUDGE OF ISRAEL: PART 2
Judges 13–16

Learning the Ways of God

Part 1 of Samson's story was quite different from any other story in the Bible. An angel visited a family to announce God was giving them a special son, Samson, who would have superpowers. God had a plan for Samson to use these powers to get revenge on the Philistines, an enemy of Israel. While he loved God, Samson was not very good at following God's commandments. However, God used Samson's faults to help fight the Philistines.

For example, Samson married a daughter of his enemy; then, he got angry because his wife spoiled his riddle and retaliated by killing thirty people. While he later realized his reaction was wrong, God used this as an opportunity to start a battle against the enemy, which Samson and the Philistines continued for the remainder of his life.

None of this sounds like the way God normally works. In fact, Samson was not a very moral person. However, this story illustrates how God uses our imperfections.[1] And what's this about superpowers? This whole story reads more like a dark comic book, in which the superhero tries to be good but has many faults. As with comic book stories, we cheer when Samson wins the battle against the enemy.

Certainly, we can learn a lot from Samson's story—mostly what *not* to do. But we also learn that sometimes God has a plan we do not understand; therefore, we need to be careful not to let our assumptions get in his way. But the story is not over. God continued his mysterious ways when, once again, he used Samson's faults to accomplish his (God's) purpose. We find that while Samson was ultimately punished for his mistakes, in the end, he came back to God in a mighty way.

Samson Continues to Make Mistakes

As the story continues, we find that Samson did not learn from his mistakes. Samson had a girlfriend in the Philistine city of Gaza. The Philistines were terribly frightened of Samson because every time they entered into a battle with him, they lost. Therefore, they sought ways to trap him, and when they heard about his girlfriend in Gaza, they made a plan to capture Samson.

To understand how cities were built in Old Testament times, you need to picture a fort with high walls; large gates at the center allowed people to enter and exit. The gates were as high as the city walls and so large that it would take many men working together to move them. Once the gates were shut each night, no one could get out until morning when the soldiers unlocked them. When the Philistines knew Samson was planning to spend the night in the city, they closed the gates and waited for him. That night, however, he decided to leave. He simply went to the gates and picked them up. Because he was so strong, he carried the gates as if they were no more than a small picket fence. Once again, he escaped from his enemies.

However, it was clear that Samson had a problem; he continued to fall in love with women who were not good for him. Even after his previous experiences, he still did not realize that he could not trust women who were not of his faith. In 1 Corinthians, Paul says we are not to marry outside our faith (meaning we should not marry a non-Christian).[2] Why not? If both of you do not accept Jesus as your Lord and Savior, how can you and your spouse agree on what is important? What will your children expect or think? How will you set priorities? How can God be first in your life? I am not saying couples in which only one is a Christian cannot work, but I am saying it is not what God intended.

But you can't help it if you fall in love with someone, can you? Of course you can! Love is not just a feeling. Wonderful feelings are great, but feelings are temporary. In contrast, marriage is a lifetime commitment. Many times during a marriage, feelings are not so evident. Love is a commitment to care for someone, even when feelings are not so strong. Love is a choice; all of us do things that are not so lovable at times. Love puts the other person's needs before our own. Sometimes you have to get through a difficult time because you have no other choice but to work it out together. We must love our spouse like Jesus loves us—unconditionally while never, ever giving up.[3] Read 1 Corinthians 13 for a complete understanding of how God loves us and how he expects us to love our fellow human beings, especially our spouse.

Samson and Delilah

Sometime later, Samson came to the Philistine valley of Sorek and became infatuated with another woman named Delilah. The rich men in Sorek came to Delilah and promised her great wealth if she could find out the secret of Samson's

super strength. Delilah was more interested in the riches the Philistines promised her than she was in Samson's love.

The next time Samson came to visit Delilah, she said to him, "Please tell me where your great strength is and how you may be bound to make you weak." Samson tried to ignore her pleas, but finally told her that if he were bound with seven fresh cords that had not been dried, he would become weak and be like any other man. That night as Samson lay sleeping, she tied him up with seven fresh cords. With the Philistines waiting outside of her door, she called to Samson, saying, "The Philistines are upon you, Samson." He jumped up and snapped the cords as though there was nothing there.

Delilah complained to Samson that he deceived her and begged him to tell her the truth regarding the source of his strength. Apparently, Samson thought she was just teasing him, or perhaps he was playing with her. Maybe he was more brawn than brain, or maybe he thought he could never lose against the Philistines. Regardless, the next time she asked him the source of his strength, he told her to bind him tightly with new ropes that had never been used. Once again, she followed his instructions, and once again, he snapped the ropes from his arms like thread.

Delilah really fussed at Samson for not telling her the truth. So, she pleaded with him a third time. This time he told her if she would weave seven locks of his hair and fasten it with a pin, he would lose his strength. Do you notice anything different about this version? It is clear that Delilah is getting to Samson; she was breaking him down and getting closer to the truth. Instead of talking about ropes and cords, he refers to the real source of his strength: his hair. It is hard to understand how Samson did not grasp that Delilah was trying to trap him.

Remember, the angel told Samson's mother and father that he was never to cut his hair. Because the true source of his strength came from God, the special powers were conditioned on his obedience to God's directive never to cut his hair. While Samson did not always follow God's laws, he never shared the true source of his strength with anyone. When Delilah did as Samson instructed, she once again called for the Philistines, and once again, Samson jumped up, pulled the pin from his hair, and was ready to battle his enemy.

After Samson fooled Delilah a third time, she was really upset with him. She begged him over and over to tell her the truth. Whether Samson finally wore down or actually believed that even if he told her the truth, he would still be strong, we do not know for sure. But we do know that he eventually shared everything with her, and she knew this time it was the truth. So, she told the Philistines to be ready to get Samson and bring her money.

Payment for Sins

During the night while Samson was asleep, Delilah had her servants shave his head. When morning came, Delilah called for the Philistines as she had three times before. However, this time Samson was weak, like any other man. He did not realize the Lord had departed from him. All of his superhuman strength was gone because he disobeyed God. His enemies seized him and gouged (punched) his eyes out.

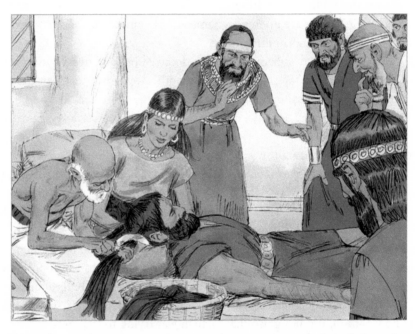

Then they took Samson to Gaza, put him in prison, and made him the city grinder. A grinder was responsible for rolling a big wheel in a circle to crush wheat to make bread for the people of the city. It was a job normally given to the oxen as it was very hard and took many hours. The people enjoyed coming by each day to see their enemy chained to a wheat grinder doing menial (lowly) work.

Samson started out with no intention of telling Delilah his real source of strength. But he continued to be with someone with whom he should have not been sharing a relationship. The Bible is clear that the people we choose to spend time with can get us into trouble and affect our relationship with God.[4] Samson slowly gave in to Delilah's request, and each time, he got a little closer to revealing the true source of his strength. In the moment, he may not have believed he would really lose his strength. Samson felt invincible—until he woke up and

realized the true source of his strength, God's power, had been removed because of his disobedience.

Falling into Satan's Trap

How does this apply to our lives? What may look like harmless fun often goes too far, and before we realize it, we are caught in a trap, no longer in control. We think one little lie will not hurt anybody, but because of the first one, we have to tell a second and a third. Soon, we can't turn back. And when we "get by" with one sin and do it a few more times without consequences, we believe we are home free to continue. But do not believe that lie because evil will creep in, sometimes inch by inch.

Satan does not come into our life like an enemy. He comes in acting like a friend, all dressed up, looking beautiful and enticing. He tells you what you want to hear. His goal is "to get a foot in the door." And once he gets you into his trap, Satan shows you the real picture—one that is ugly and devastating. Jesus reminds us that the devil comes to kill, steal, and destroy.[5] For example, because of Samson's desire for a woman's affection, he eventually violated his commitment to God. Delilah got her foot in the door by getting him to lie about where his strength came from. He likely thought,

So what if her country is my enemy? She is nice to me and so beautiful and desirable. I need her, and I will never tell her the truth.

But he does tell her. And then his friend/lover revealed herself as a true enemy. The fun was over, and Samson was left with a miserable life. What was once beautiful became ugly, and Samson was no longer in control. We believe we are smarter than Samson and would never fall into such a trap, but we are naïve to think we could resist. When we do fall, God may leave us to our own devices to overcome the problem we created.[6]

Let me share a personal story to show how subtle Satan can be. When I was thirteen, my mother and father would not let me go to a new Doris Day movie. Until that movie came out, she was known to play in only wholesome movies. But this one was advertised as more risqué than any she had been in before. My parents thought I was too young to watch it, so I was not allowed to go. Twenty years later, while my mother was visiting my home, we watched a movie together with my family. Yes, it was the same movie I was not allowed to see twenty years earlier. And during the movie, my mother said, "It is too bad they do not make cute movies like this anymore."

You see, over twenty years, movies had changed so much that what she once considered too risqué to watch was now "wholesome." But the changes in entertainment evolved so subtly that we did not even realize it was happening. And that's how we find ourselves in Satan's trap. This example is one we can laugh at, but do not miss the message that the enemy's plan is to change your perspective to his. And, it is evident in today's society that Satan's plan is working.

One day, our lax standards will cause God to leave us to our own destruction, in hopes we will turn back to him. In the meantime, we will lose our source of *his* power. The United States of America was founded on the principle that we are (were) "one Nation under God," but this country has largely abandoned this concept in exchange for what society now claims is right and fair—no matter that it is an abomination to God. I will share much more about this in my next story.

Each of us likely remembers a time we started out not wanting to do wrong, but because of a friend or a circumstance or a feeling, our belief that the action was wrong shifted, and we decided it was okay to continue. If it has not caught you yet, it soon may. Illegal drugs are a good example. Using starts out as fun and exciting; but soon it turns ugly, and we find ourselves out of control. Or worse, we are under Satan's control.

Evaluate your life and purge whatever you need to remove before it is too late. Samson paid dearly. We, too, may get caught and pay dearly. However, we can be comforted in one significant way. No matter the consequences we have to deal with, we can learn from Samson's final days that God never totally abandons us.

Samson's Revenge

Not too much later, the Philistines came to Gaza to celebrate their great victory over Samson and to offer sacrifices to their god, Dagon. While the celebration was in high gear, they decided it would be fun to bring Samson to the arena so they could gloat over their fallen, pitiful foe. Samson was taken from the grinder and brought before the people in the coliseum. Since Samson was blind, he asked the young man who brought him to the coliseum to let him rest his hands on the main pillars of the building. There he prayed to God to allow him to have his strength back one last time so that he could avenge his enemies.

Since Samson had been chained up for some time, his hair had begun to grow back. God answered his prayer and gave him back his strength. He pushed on the two pillars as hard as he could, and the coliseum fell in. All the people in the arena were killed that day, including Samson. The coliseum was full; there were even three thousand people on the roof. Samson killed more of his enemy that day than in all other battles combined. It was a great victory for God and sweet revenge for Samson. Throughout Samson's life, God used this man's weakness and imperfections to accomplish his purposes.[7]

This story shows how effectively God can use those of us who are far from perfect and not doing everything the way we should. However, we learn that God will not always protect us if we continue to be disobedient to his commandments. Like Samson, we must be prepared to pay the consequences of our sins—even if we escape punishment for many years. More than anything, this story should teach us how *not* to act. And too, Samson's story teaches us that no matter how disobediently we act, God will return to us once we repent and ask for his forgiveness. God never, ever gives up on us, so let's not give up on him.

For Further Discussion
- How does Samson compare with all of the superheroes we read about in comic books and see in today's movies? Why are we so enamored with superheroes?
- What have you learned *not* to do because of the lessons from Samson's story?
- How can God's love manifested in *you* make a difference in your love for your spouse and your commitment to your marriage?

- How can God's love for you affect all aspects of your life and, in turn, provide opportunities for you to help others?
- Have you let the world teach you things that go against what God says through the Bible? Has your stance weakened or even changed because of what society now says is acceptable?
- Since Samson was disobedient, why do you think God allowed Samson to get revenge?

For Further Study

1. 2 Corinthians 12:5–6—We should boast in our weaknesses, not in our human strengths; it would be foolishness to God.
2. 1 Corinthians 7:39—We are cautioned by Paul to only marry another Christian.
3. 1 Corinthians 13:1–13—God's explanation of the importance of love in all aspects of our lives.
4. 2 Corinthians 6:14–15—Do not develop formal relationships with unbelievers, for how can there be a partnership between righteousness and lawlessness, or what fellowship has light with darkness? Or what harmony has Christ with Belial (another name for the devil), or what has a believer in common with an unbeliever?
5. John 10:10—The thief (the devil) comes only to kill, steal, and destroy.
6. 1 Corinthians 5:5—I have decided to deliver such a one to Satan for the destruction of his flesh so that his spirit may be saved in the day of the Lord Jesus.
7. 2 Corinthians 12:9—Paul told the Corinthians that God said to him, "My grace is sufficient for you, for power is perfected in weakness." And then he added, "Most gladly, therefore, I would rather boast about my weaknesses so that the power of Christ may dwell in me."

Chapter 10
TYRANNY AND EVIL REIGN IN ISRAEL
Judges 17–21

The period of the judges should have been an exciting time for the Israelites. And there were stretches of time during which they served God and worshipped him in ways that pleased him. However, too often, the times were characterized by self-indulgence and ignoring their commitment to God. This ultimately resulted in God allowing the Israelites to wallow in their own sins, followed by oppression from their enemies. It's a wonder God included some of these stories in the Bible. But, as I hope you have learned from the earlier stories, even the sad, despicable tales of woe deliver a message from God. Throughout history, we have seen humans suffer when they chose to be disobedient to God's Word and follow their own paths, eventually leading to self-destruction. I believe the stories in this chapter are a warning for the world today.

A word of caution: This is a story of immorality and violent actions. While I believe it has a powerful message, I recommend you pre-read the story before deciding whether the timing is right to read as a family.

This era where God's people chose to follow their own way is referred to as the period of apostasy. It is truly a sad time in the history of the Jewish nation. Like the Israelites during this period, I believe we, too, are making the same mistakes today, and we will suffer greatly for choosing a pattern of behavior contrary to the principles God has laid forth.

Every Man Did What Was Right in His Own Eyes
The writer of the Book of Judges repeatedly used the phrase, "Every man did what was right in his own eyes," in referring to this period of apostasy. And when men follow what they think is right—even with good intentions—it often leads

to failure; evil creeps in and ultimately takes control. The following story is an example of the evil that results when mankind follows what they think is right.

Micah, a man from the tribe of Ephraim, stole 1,100 pieces of silver from his mother. Later, he felt bad about his misconduct, so he returned the silver to her and made graven images for household idols. While being sorry for stealing was clearly an admirable change of heart, breaking the second of God's Ten Commandments (you shall not make for yourself idols or graven images) was an intolerable act before God. It is amazing to me that Micah thought his behavior honored God. But then, I am equally amazed that many church leaders today accept certain activities that are unmistakably against God's specific commandments while other Christians validate lifestyles in clear violation of God's creation. Micah's actions were only the beginning of the inexcusable deeds.

Sometime later, a Levite man came to visit Micah, who requested that the Levite become the priest to his household. He agreed and became like one of his sons. A few years later, Israelites from the tribe of Dan passed by Micah's house looking for a new territory for their tribe. The men asked Micah's priest to inquire of God regarding their efforts, and he discovered they would be successful in their quest to find a new home. The men continued on their journey and found an ideal place.

After returning to their families, they enthusiastically shared how they could easily take over a territory where some peaceful members of another tribe lived. Apparently, taking land owned by a distant relative was not considered evil by the society of that day. As the warriors from the tribe of Dan headed to take over the new land, they passed by Micah's house again. This time, they stole Micah's household idols and graven images.

When Micah's priest questioned what the men were doing, they told him to be silent. And furthermore, they requested that he join them by saying, "Wouldn't it be better for you to be priest for an entire tribe than one family?" The priest agreed and gladly joined the Danites; he conveniently remained silent about the stolen idols and graven images. Clearly, he felt no loyalty to Micah, his "adopted father," who had treated him like a son.

The army of Dan then entered the peaceful village and easily wiped out the families who lived there. The Danites reestablished their home and called it the city of Dan. Micah's priest and his descendants served the tribe for many years. The Danites and Micah's priest were doing "what was right in their own eyes." From *their* perspective they were following God.

Why would God allow such a thing among his Chosen People? God had often warned the people to follow his commandments, but they refused to listen. However, before we criticize the Israelites, let's consider if what the tribe of Dan did is any different from what we, as Americans, did in taking over our land from the Native Americans. At first, our forefathers wanted to share the land, but later, they took over and forced the Native Americans to live on reservations if they wanted to stay as a tribe. And too, don't we worship "idols" that are contrary to the Word of God? For example, we put people, such as movie stars, sports heroes, and rock musicians, on a pedestal, or we spend far too much time on games, such as fantasy football, Minecraft, and World of Warcraft, to name a few. Admiring the lives of these famous people or enjoying games is not evil; however, spending too much time focused on them, with little or no attention to God, is wrong. If we are not careful, those fascinations become our idols when we, in essence, worship them instead of God.

So many things we do seem right to us, but God understands better than we do what is good. Satan takes what God establishes as truth and makes slight changes so that it still seems right; this is called counterfeiting.[1] We are fooled into thinking something is real or true and believing we are doing "right," but in the end, it will lead to our downfall. As our society grows further from God, it becomes more difficult for us to maintain an accurate "measuring rod" to discern what God teaches regarding right and wrong.

Evil Takes Over

The next story is even worse; we are not even given names for these people. A certain Levite's wife left him for another man; then she decided to go to her father's house in Bethlehem. Her husband wanted her back, so he went to his father-in-law's house and talked her into returning home. On their way home, they entered a city in the land of Benjamin. An older man told the Levite that it would be dangerous for them to sleep in the open square and invited the couple to stay with him.

That night, certain "worthless" men of the city pounded on the old man's door and demanded that the Levite be given to them so that they could sexually abuse him. The old man pleaded with the men,

> *Please do not act so wickedly, as he is a guest in my house; I am responsible to protect him. Do not commit this act of folly.*

The old man even offered his virgin daughter as a substitute. The law in their society said that women were not as important as was his requirement to take care of his male guest.

But the men would not listen to the old man. In an effort to save the day, the Levite's wife was pushed out of the house, and the door was shut. The worthless men raped and abused her, then let her go just before dawn. The woman struggled to get back to the old man's house and died at his doorstep. When her husband arose in the morning and opened the door, he said to her, "Get up and let's go." But there was no answer. When he realized she was dead, he was furious.

The Levite was so angry that he cut her into twelve pieces and sent one piece to each of the twelve tribes with a note explaining what a despicable act had occurred. The people of Israel said nothing like this had ever happened since they had come from the land of Egypt. All of Israel came together to punish the men who committed this act and demanded the people of Benjamin deliver the worthless fellows to be judged as murderers, thus removing this wickedness from Israel. But the sons of Benjamin would not listen to the voice of their fellow Israelite families. As a result, each side prepared for battle, precipitating civil war.

God's people finally decided it was time to turn to him for guidance. Phinehas sought God's counsel to ensure the victory for Israel over the sons of Benjamin. So great was their victory that twenty-five thousand Benjamites were killed. The Israelites allowed six hundred men to live so that the tribe of Benjamin would not be totally wiped out.

Who's in Control: God or Man?

While evil has raised its ugly head throughout human history, I believe the door opens much wider to sin when man abandons God's ways and decides to follow "what seems right in his own eyes." Why else would the Levite accept his wife being raped and abused and then be so terribly offended when he learned they killed her? It's as if he allowed them to use his property but not destroy it. Women should never be thought of as property. And too, why would the Benjamites support family members who were so horribly vicious and vile?

It is clear to me that these events were a result of ignoring God for many years. One slight change led to another until eventually their standards and lifestyles were out of control. This became Israel's pattern of behavior. Throughout God's relationship with his people, he continually warned them what would happen if they did not follow his laws. However, when man insists on his own way, God will let him fall into the devil's trap.

While we, in today's society, would not condone the actions of these worthless men or the Benjamites, I believe we have to take responsibility for contributing to the lack of morals that exist today in our world and, in particular, in the United States. "We the People" have allowed our government to decide that we can no longer use God's commandments as a standard when making our laws. The separation of church and state envisioned by our forefathers never intended for us to leave God out of our lives and our laws; Rather, their intent was to prevent "the church" from dictating what government should do.

To demonstrate how strongly our founding fathers felt about using God's standards as a basis for making laws, I offer the following quote from John Jay, the United States' First Chief Justice of the Supreme Court (1789–1795). Keep in mind, his view was the prevailing belief of most who ratified our constitution:

> *No human society has ever been able to maintain both order and freedom, both cohesiveness and liberty apart from the moral precepts of the Christian religion . . . Should our republic ever forget this fundamental precept of government, this great experiment [our new nation] will then be surely doomed.*

Therefore, what was acceptable for the first two hundred years of our existence is now considered unconstitutional. Laws that our government originally established are now being abolished.

When man begins to allow society to determine what is right, it is the beginning of the end for that society. Many of the laws men make sound reasonable and fair, but God sees our needs and understands our weaknesses. We need to accept our limitations and allow God's way to rule. Man is too self-centered and highly influenced by what society thinks is right. As I shared earlier, Satan counterfeits the truth to make it appear fair and reasonable. He is the ruler of this world,[2] and Satan wants us to follow his standard so that he can kill, steal, and destroy; our sinful nature has made us easy prey for the roaring lion that he is.[3]

Following a Moral Standard

There has to be some moral standard, some standard of measure to guide man, that can stand the test of time; otherwise, our society will continue to follow the morals of the day. Today, we would be horrified by what people thought was wrong hundreds of years ago. And our founding fathers would be horrified by what we think is "right." Originally, our federal and state governments used the Bible as the moral standard. But today's society has decided that the original standard is outdated and not inclusive for all people. Our society says, "We're doing it for the good of mankind," but in reality, we are doing what "man thinks is good in his own eyes."

Our foolishness shines forth when we choose any standard other than God's Word. Even though our society condemns the recent increase in violence, especially the horrid killings in our high schools and public places, I am concerned that we have indirectly encouraged it by our tolerance and acceptance for "free thinking," *without a standard to measure against.* And too, our headstrong direction to eliminate God from all of our laws and public gatherings has contributed to our immorality.

Nevertheless, we do not need to be naïve. Having our laws return to God's standard will not eliminate the evil in our world, nor will it stop people from sinning. Israel's story is an undeniable testimony to this. They were given the Law of Moses directly from God, yet they were constantly living in sin. God expected this, but he also expected them to recognize their faults and come to him in repentance.

Even before our nation's laws eliminated God and his ways, there was much sin in our country. The difference is that in the past, we called actions contrary to the teachings in the Bible "sin," and society frowned upon these actions. Now, we call these actions "alternative lifestyles" and have concluded we have no right to enforce God's ways on people. As a result, we are left without a measuring rod, choosing instead to go with "what we think is right."

None of this should imply that fifty to sixty years ago, or even at any time in history, mankind has had it right. For example, while in my lifetime we have allowed our society to turn away from God in many ways, we have learned that we were, and still are, prejudiced in many ungodly ways. Our laws have rightly been adjusted to reflect these injustices. However, in truth, mankind has no clue

what is right. And until we choose to live by God's standard, like John Jay said, we are "doomed."

Are you willing to stand for God? Can you say enough is enough?

But what can one person do? I realize it is neither popular nor easy to stand up against the government, the media, and those in positions of influence. But at some point, we must take a stand like Phinehas did in this story when he pleaded for God's deliverance and victory. God honored him, and evil was once again wiped out.

When we follow God and endure to the end, we, too, can be assured of the final victory.[4] But as I have shared before, we must all be willing to put away our selfish ways and rely on the Holy Spirit within us to hear rightly from God. It will be difficult for us to come to agreement with all the variety of viewpoints and personalities. It cannot truly happen until Jesus returns and rules as king. But we can do better and recognize that God is the only way.

If we are to make a difference, we must show society—through our own life and actions—that God's laws are good for mankind. God was not trying to be mean or punish people when he gave us his commandments. God's laws provide protection, safety, and a certain sense of morality that society needs if we are to live in harmony and favor with God and man. God's standards have never changed. Jesus changed the presentation of God's message into a more loving format, but God's laws, founded in mercy, love, and grace, have never wavered. I believe it is our obligation to influence young people by holding God's standard for them to follow.

Too often today, Christians stand up in ways that are not God-like; they stand according to their own self-righteousness. As Christians, we must be careful to avoid the mistake of "doing what is right in our own eyes" but instead be under the guidance of the Holy Spirit. I believe we should start by working on the hearts of the people. Once people turn back to God, then our government should follow.

For Further Discussion

- Have you ever considered that what you think is right might not be the same as what God thinks?
- Discuss areas where you believe society or government laws differ from what you believe. What about where God and society disagree?
- Why do you think God and society are so different in what and how they think? What role, if any, do you think Satan (the devil) plays in these differences?
- From all of the recordings at the time, it is clear that our founding fathers wanted God to be a consideration when we make laws to govern our country. Originally, the Bible was used to support many of our federal and state laws. Why has the government changed so much from these early days?
- Do you agree with my point that we are now basing our laws on the same principle the Bible says was at work in the Book of Judges: "Every man did what was right in his own eyes"?

For Further Study

1. Ephesians 6:12—For our struggle (battle) is not against flesh and blood, but against spiritual forces of wickedness in heavenly places.
2. John 14:30—Referring to Satan, Jesus said, "The ruler of this world is coming, and he has nothing in me" (meaning Jesus was without sin).
3. We need to understand and respect the fact that the devil has power:
   a. 1 Peter 5:8—Your adversary, the devil, prowls around like a roaring lion, seeking someone to devour.
   b. John 10:10—The thief (the devil) comes to kill, steal, and destroy.

4. 1 Corinthians 15:55–57—Death is swallowed up in victory. Thanks be to God, who gives us the victory through our Lord, Jesus Christ.

Chapter 11
RUTH, A STORY OF LOVE, ROMANCE, AND REDEMPTION: PART 1
Ruth 1–4

Ruth is one of two books in the Bible named after a woman and is primarily the story of Ruth, Naomi (Ruth's mother-in-law), and Boaz, a man who rescued them. Ruth is a short story that is different from any other book in the Bible—it is about ordinary folks living ordinary lives and struggling to exist in a very difficult world. Even more unusual is that Ruth is not an Israelite. The Old Testament is almost exclusively about God's Chosen Family, the Israelites. So, why is there an entire book named after a Gentile (someone who is not Jewish)? Let's see if we can discover the special significance of this story, God's "good news" for all of us.

The story of Ruth takes place during the period of the judges, but in this story we find nothing about the leaders fighting or their enemy. This story teaches us about a family that bonds together through all the trials and tribulations of life; furthermore, it is a tale of love, romance, and redemption with a happy ending.

Personally, Ruth is one of my favorite stories in the Bible; first, because it is about people just like you and me. Everything does not always go well for them, and they must learn to live with the difficult circumstances in which they find themselves. This is a story of encouragement from God, who cares even when it doesn't always seem like he does. God's plan is to take these ordinary folks and make them extraordinary because of their willingness to be obedient to his law and his Word.

Second, it's not just the main storyline that makes the book of Ruth so special; more than any other book in the Old Testament, the story lays out God's plan for mankind. God clearly demonstrates that he is not concerned only with the Israelites; he cares for each and every one of us. Through Ruth's story, we can see God's plans unfold for the Israelites and the Gentiles. Yes, God has a plan even for those who do not know him. We can all be part of God's Chosen Family. It is beautiful to learn there was love, romance, and redemption for these ordinary people, but I hope you will see the even greater message about God's love, romance, and redemption for you and me. I pray I can bring this story alive for each of you as Dr. M. R. DeHaan did for me forty-five years ago.

The Family Immediately Faces Difficulties

Now, it came about in the days when the judges governed, there was a famine in the land. Elimelech, a man of Bethlehem in Judah, left his country to find food for his family. He settled in the land of Moab with his wife, Naomi, and their two sons, Mahlon and Chilion. In Moab, his sons found wives named Orpah and Ruth. Sadly, Elimelech died and soon after so did both sons before either had children. In her lost and distressed state, Naomi decided to return to Bethlehem. Since the famine was over in Israel, she hoped her relatives would help her.

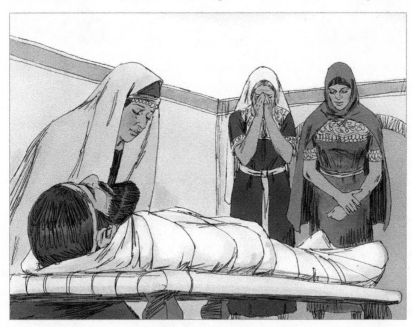

She urged her daughters-in-law to stay near their families because they were young enough to find new husbands, but both so admired Naomi that they wanted to go with her. While Orpah finally decided to return home to her family, Ruth insisted that she would be better off staying with her mother-in-law. In spite of all the difficulties Naomi encountered, there was something different that made her special, and Ruth was able to see it.

Ruth summed up her feelings when she made one of the more profound statements in the Bible:

Do not urge me to leave you; for where you go, I will go. Your people shall be my people and your God my God.

I am sure Naomi was a wonderful person, but the more important point in her declaration was that Ruth chose to follow Naomi's God. We know him to be the one and only true God. Though she did not know it then, this risky decision would take Ruth from being a poor and lowly member of society to a person who now ranks as one of the most revered women in the entire Bible. And I believe she has a special place reserved for her in heaven. I believe that Orpah was also nice, but her fatal choice to return home may have been her doom. Do you need to join Ruth and choose to follow the one and only true God?

Returning Home

Bethlehem was all abuzz when word got out that Naomi returned home. In her distress, she told her friends of the devastation and loss she had endured while her family was in Moab, saying, "I went out full, but the Lord has brought me back empty." She continued, "Do not call me Naomi; call me Mara, for the Almighty has dealt very bitterly with me." She felt lonely and forgotten—even by her God. But she did not give up; she held a thread of hope by trusting in the provision that the Law of Moses established for widows. In return, we will see that God provided for her beyond her wildest dreams. So, even when you are discouraged with life, keep a thread of hope alive that God cares for you. Do you have struggles? Then seek God for answers and allow his provisions to meet your needs. He will respond beyond anything you can imagine, but perhaps not when or how you expect him to. Let's see how this story can be an encouragement for you.

As it turned out, Naomi and Ruth returned to Bethlehem in the middle of the harvest season. We now get to see another of God's special laws that was put into place for widows and strangers (foreigners). God gave specific instructions to the land owners during the harvest season. The workers were not to harvest the corners of the fields. Furthermore, if workers dropped grain in the field, they were not allowed to pick it up. As the Law of Moses dictated, these were "gleanings" designated for foreigners and needy widows who had no sons to take care of them.[1]

Because Naomi was old and tired, Ruth offered to go to the fields to see what small amount of grain she could gather for the two of them. As it happened, Ruth came upon a field owned by a man named Boaz, who was a godly and righteous man. When he saw the young woman resting with the other harvesters, he asked who she was. Boaz learned she was Naomi's daughter-in-law and that she had been working very hard all day long to gather grain.

Boaz was extremely impressed that this young woman would work so hard in the fields on behalf of her mother-in-law. He recognized her unselfish act and wanted to reward her, so he told Ruth to stay in his fields for the full harvest season. Ruth was an attractive foreigner with no one to protect her, and Boaz was concerned some immoral men would take advantage of her. He gave his supervisors specific instructions to make sure no one harmed her. Further, he told them to drop some grain on purpose so that it would be hers to pick up; he wanted to make sure Ruth had plenty to take home to Naomi. Boaz also gave her food to eat so that she would have the strength to work the full day. He even gave her enough that she would have extra to take home for Naomi's supper.

You can imagine how surprised and excited Naomi was when Ruth came home with food. She was also amazed at how much grain Ruth was able to harvest. As instructed, the workers dropped extra bundles of grain for Ruth. Naomi immediately knew that something special happened and wanted to know all the details of the day. Could it be that their luck had turned around? Could it be that she was no longer "Mara," but once again Naomi? Naomi was even more excited when she learned Boaz owned the field that Ruth had harvested from; for you see, Boaz was a near kinsman to Naomi. We will soon see why that relationship is so important.

A Plan of Redemption

Naomi now had a plan. She had seen the kindness of Boaz, and she knew the Law of Moses. She was hopeful that Boaz would help them, not only for this harvest season but for a lifetime. Naomi's previous concern was that Ruth would not be able to marry and have someone take care of her—but maybe Boaz would be willing to help. She was confident that the kindness he had already shown Ruth was evidence that he would do the right thing.

As you may recall from an earlier story in Volume 1, "The Sons of Jacob," a wife whose husband died before they had any children married her brother-in-law; his children by this wife would receive the inheritance of the deceased brother.[2] This was now part of the Law of Moses.[3] The obligation fell to the nearest kinsman. While Naomi knew she was too old to have children, she was hopeful that Boaz would take Ruth as a substitute and "redeem" her according to the law. Because Ruth was not an Israelite, Boaz would not likely think of redeeming Ruth through marriage; therefore, Naomi had to set the plan in motion for Ruth to make the request.

Naomi instructed Ruth to bathe, put on perfume, and dress in her best clothes. She was to go to the threshing floor and follow Naomi's instructions:

Do not make yourself known; stay hidden until night falls and all the men are asleep. Then watch where Boaz lies down for the night. Once you are sure everyone is asleep, uncover Boaz's feet and lay there until the night air wakes him up.

Ruth agreed to do all that Naomi requested, and it happened just as Naomi said it would. Boaz awoke and was startled to see a young woman at his feet. "Who are you?" he asked. She answered, "I am Ruth, so spread your covering over your maid, for you are a close relative." Back then, if you were a widow with no son, this was the way the law provided for you to ask a man to marry you. Ruth had taken a big risk. What if Boaz said no and was upset with her? After all, she was a Gentile, and Israelites were generally not allowed to marry outside the Chosen Family. Would you have been bold enough to go to the threshing floor and make such a risky request?

Boaz spoke quietly,

May you be blessed by God, my daughter. You have shown even greater kindness than your hard work in the fields. For you could have gone after a much younger man. Yet you were obedient to your mother-in-law's needs by asking to be her substitute. I will do whatever you ask, for all of my people know that you are a woman of excellence.

Wow! What a great confirmation and compliment to Ruth. However, there was one more hoop to jump through. As it turned out, Boaz was not the closest relative.[4] So before Boaz could redeem Ruth as a substitute for Naomi, he first had to find out if his relative would take responsibility. Boaz promised Ruth he would be pleased to marry her if the closest living relative did not.

Boaz was also careful to protect Ruth's reputation; thus, he told her to remain at his feet for the night. Before the sun rose, she was to return home so no one would think Ruth had come to lay with him. To ensure Naomi would know he was willing to take on the obligation, Boaz gave Ruth his cloak filled with fresh grain.

What a long night for Naomi! Imagine her thoughts as she waited. Did she have a chance for a new life? Was God really showing her mercy by having her family redeemed by a rich man? Was she really so lucky to have a Gentile daughter-in-law who was willing to sacrifice her own needs for her mother-in-law? Was the promise of God's love and redemption real? To find out, she would have to wait out the night.

Nights can be scary and seem to last such a long time. Have you ever stayed awake at night worrying about something? Or maybe you've been excited yet afraid a special event would not happen as you wanted it to. We, too, have to be patient and wait on God's timing. Are you willing?

To further elaborate on this picture, the night Ruth went to visit Boaz, she laid at his feet. When he awoke, she was redeemed, just as Jesus was raised from the dead (he awoke), and we, too, were redeemed. Ruth lay safely at the feet of Boaz for the remainder of the night, just as the church lies safely at the feet of Jesus until he returns. Boaz gave his promise, but Naomi had to wait out the night to learn his answer. The story parallels how Israel today must wait, for they, too, are to be redeemed but are in the dark for now.

Ruth, a Gentile slave, found a redeemer[5] because she was associated with Naomi. Even more, not only was Ruth redeemed, but she also became the bride of a rich man who provided for all of her needs. As I will describe in more detail in part 2 of Ruth's story, this is a beautiful picture of God's plan for all mankind. As the New Testament describes, a bride is symbolic of the church, with Jesus as the Groom.[6] Just as Boaz was the husband/redeemer of Ruth, the Gentile, so is Jesus the Bridegroom/Redeemer/Messiah of what the New Testament calls the Gentile church. With redemption, the church, like Ruth, becomes the new bride.

In this metaphor, Naomi is like Israel in today's world; Israel has been put on hold. The Gentile church now holds the place as the family of God, just as Ruth held the place for Naomi. Once Ruth had a son, Naomi and her heirs could also be redeemed. Without a son, Naomi would have no heir to receive the inheritance and, therefore, no reason to redeem the land. Naomi was back in her home country, but the land had not been restored to her. She needed to wait on her redeemer, Boaz, to marry the bride, Ruth, and produce a son before she (Naomi) could have her land restored to her family. So, too, through the Son (Jesus), one day Israel will be restored to the family of God.

In part 2 of Ruth's story, we will learn how Naomi's future unfolds. In the meantime, are you beginning to see how this story lays out God's redemptive plan for you and me?

For Further Discussion

- Have you ever lost a member of your family? Was the loss devastating?
- Does someone in your family have needs beyond which you can provide?
- Can you think of ways God provides for us today like he did with the gleanings for widows and foreigners?

- Are you waiting for something exciting? How difficult is it to wait?
- Do you get scared at night? Are you afraid of the dark? Humans have a natural fear of the dark that we should honor and that God wants us to be careful of. The Bible describes Jesus as the Light and says Satan rules the Domain of Darkness.

For Further Study

1. Leviticus 19:9–10—An owner of the land was not allowed to harvest the corner of the fields nor could their workers pick up any grain that they dropped (called gleanings); this part of the harvest was for the needy, widows, and foreigners.
2. Genesis 38:7–8—Judah's son, Onan, was required to marry Tamar, the wife of Onan's brother, Er, who died; Onan was told to raise up children with Tamar.
3. Deuteronomy 25:5–10—The brother of one who is deceased must marry the dead brother's wife and raise up children with her if she had no children when her husband died. These children would then receive the inheritance of the deceased brother.
4. Leviticus 25:25—The nearest kinsman must have the first chance to redeem the property of one who became so poor he had to sell his land.
5. Leviticus 25:47–49—A Jewish slave may be redeemed by a near kinsman.
6. Jesus and his church are presented symbolically in the New Testament as the husband and wife and the bride and the bridegroom:
   a. Revelation 21:9—The bride, the wife of the Lamb (Jesus)
   b. Ephesians 5:23–27—The husband is head of the wife, just as Christ is head of the church.
   c. John 3:28–29—John the Baptist declares that the person, the Christ (the Messiah), who comes after him will be the Bridegroom who receives the bride (the church).

Chapter 12

RUTH, A STORY OF LOVE, ROMANCE, AND REDEMPTION: PART 2

Ruth 1–4

In part 1 of Ruth's Story, we learned about the difficulties Ruth and Naomi faced. Ruth found herself gathering barley in the fields of Boaz, a rich relative of Naomi. Though Ruth and Naomi did not know it at the time, this was the beginning of a miracle. Boaz was impressed with Ruth's willingness to take care of Naomi, her mother-in-law. We learned that under the Law of Moses, Ruth, through her deceased husband Mahlon, could request that Boaz redeem the land Naomi's family lost; furthermore, Ruth could ask Boaz to marry her. When Ruth made the request, Boaz agreed so long as their closer relative, who had first choice, would not agree to redeem her.

God's Provision Saves

Can you imagine Ruth and Naomi's excitement as Ruth shared all the events of the night? Boaz wasted no time. The next morning, he went to the city gates where all important transactions took place. When the closer relative arrived, Boaz asked him to step aside and hear his opportunity. Boaz asked ten other men to be witnesses to the transaction. Boaz shared,

Naomi lost the land that belongs to our relative Elimelech. You have the first right to redeem the property. If you do not, I will.

Boaz's relative agreed to redeem Naomi's property until Boaz told him he would be obligated to marry Ruth. The relative was willing to redeem the property and take Naomi. However, he would not redeem Ruth as part of the deal; I believe he was afraid any children he and Ruth had together would somehow jeopardize his family's inheritance – according to the Law of Moses, his children with Ruth would receive an inheritance as if they were Mahlon's children (Ruth's first husband). As a result, the relative told Boaz, "You may have my right, for I am not willing to redeem Ruth."

Boaz declared to the ten elders, "You are witnesses today that I have purchased from the hand of Naomi all that belongs to Elimelech and all that belongs to Chilion and Mahlon. Moreover, I have acquired Ruth the Moabite as the widow of Mahlon to be my wife and to raise up the inheritance of the deceased." All of the people in the court of the city were impressed with the actions of Boaz. He had given up his inheritance to Naomi's husband and son. The people responded, "May the Lord make Ruth like Rachel and Leah and provide you a family that will make you wealthy and famous in all of Bethlehem."

So, Boaz took Ruth as his wife, and soon she gave him a son named Obed. Then, the women of the city came to Naomi and declared,

> *Blessed is the Lord who has given you a Redeemer. May he also take care of you and your family in your old age to come. And blessed are you to have Ruth as your daughter-in-law, who loves you and is better than seven sons.*

We need to understand how dramatic this statement was. In Bible times, having sons made the woman important and successful. As the women explained, the son became the redeemer. In the same way, Jesus, God's Son, is our Redeemer.

Naomi took the child and laid him in her lap. What a transition! Two women in poverty, with no expectation of relief, were rewarded with both material security and a son to ensure their legacy. We will see later in the story just how special Ruth's son was. Just as God did for Ruth and Naomi, he is gracious and faithful to reward us and, when necessary, forgive us. All he asks in return is that we stay with him through all the trials of life. Similar to Ruth's declaration to Naomi before they returned to Naomi's homeland, we need to declare to God, "For where you go, I will go. Your people shall be my people and you will be my God."

It should be plain to see the kindness and love in this story. First, Ruth, for the love of her mother-in-law, was willing to give up everything to follow Naomi and her God. Ruth was rewarded for her willingness to work so hard for Naomi when she received kindness from Boaz. He courted Ruth by giving her food, protection, and even a special blessing by telling the men to drop extra bundles of grain in the field. A romance developed as Ruth came to him in the night and offered to become his wife. He graciously accepted her invitation of marriage, and according to the law, he agreed to redeem her; that is, he bought her out of the bondage of poverty. Ruth was adopted into the house of Israel as a free woman.

However, love stories always seem to have a twist. There was one more hurdle that had to be cleared; a closer relative still had first choice in the redemption of Naomi's land. Yet, as with all true love stories, there was a happy ending when the closer relative was not willing to marry Ruth as part of the redemption. Not only were Boaz and Ruth rewarded, Naomi also received a son whom she could call her own as Ruth's gift to Naomi. As a result, Obed became Naomi's legacy. What a blessing from God!

Portrait of Christ, the Church, and the Future of Israel

But the personal relationship between Ruth and Naomi is just part of the storyline. As I introduced in part 1, Ruth's story reveals God's redemptive plan for all of mankind. When we look for God's message for us in the story, we can see Boaz as a picture of Jesus, with Ruth representing the church/the body of Christ, and Naomi representing Israel.

The story began with Israel in a time of famine. As we learned in the twenty-eighth chapter of Deuteronomy, a famine would occur when Israel was not following God's commandments; thus, the Israelites would be under a curse until they were delivered by the mercy of God. Israel was like Naomi when she returned and declared to her friends, "The Lord has turned against me, and the Almighty has afflicted me."

Ruth was a Gentile, as was anyone who was not an Israelite; she was hopelessly lost as a sinner without a Savior and was outside of God's family.[1] But by grace, she was brought into the family. Boaz graciously accepted her as a substitute for Naomi, which is much like what Jesus did when God's Chosen Family rejected him, and he turned to the undeserving Gentiles to create his new family (the church/the body of Christ).

"Grace" is a new term introduced by Paul and Peter in the New Testament. Grace is a gift of love from God, even though we do not deserve it.[2] Why don't we deserve God's love? Not only are we not perfect, but we also fail to follow his commandments. We are selfish and do what we want, instead of all he has called us to do. Yet, God loved us so much that he sent his only son into the world to take the punishment for us such that all who believe in him shall have eternal life.[3] So while we were still sinners, Jesus died and rose to save us.[4] That is a gift worth praising God about. It is grace abounding.

Boaz was Ruth's savior in the same way that Jesus is the Savior of the Gentiles. Like the Gentiles, Ruth was no longer separated from God; the church, like Ruth, is now God's family. Naomi and her family forfeited their inheritance when they left for other lands; without Ruth, Naomi had no possibility of a son to redeem her property. Boaz redeemed them (Ruth, the property, and as a result, Naomi, too), and under the Law, Ruth's son by Boaz was considered to be Mahlon's (Ruth's first husband; Naomi's son). So, just as Naomi found redemption through Ruth, Israel will find its way back to God through the church when Israel accepts Jesus as Savior.[5] What a powerful concept! You may want to take a moment to review each thought and let this sink in.

Under Jewish Law, property, widows, and slaves could be redeemed,[6] but only by a kinsman (a relative) who was willing to pay the price. We found that Naomi's late husband had a kinsman who was a closer relative than Boaz; however, he (the closer relative) was not willing to pay the price, which included accepting Ruth as his bride. Boaz, like Jesus, was rich enough to pay the price and was willing to share his inheritance, first with Ruth and then later with Naomi when the son was born.

Mankind's Inability to Save Himself

What part did this "closer relative" play? Jesus was not only man, but also God.[7] He is a relative, but not in the same manner as our earthly relatives because he was "begotten" from God; and therefore, born without our sin nature. Man had failed in his attempt to reclaim what Adam lost; he was not capable of redeeming himself, much less all of mankind. So mankind needed a Savior, but according to the law established by God, the Savior had to be a man. Since Jesus shared "flesh and blood" (humanity), he was both willing and able to redeem us because he lived a sinless life making his death a perfect sacrifice; thereby becoming a faithful and merciful high priest making his request before God.[8] Thus, our "Kinsman-Redeemer" reconciled us to God.[9]

Remember, from the beginning, God had a plan to redeem all of mankind. He was just concentrating on one family (Israel) to provide the way. Through Ruth's story, God reminds us that his plan includes everyone. The bride/the church/the Gentiles would become God's family until Israel could be restored. And this is where we find ourselves today; the Gentile church is now God's family, waiting for the right time to restore Israel.

To put all of these events in perspective, Boaz is a picture of our Kinsman-Redeemer, Jesus, who was willing and able to pay the price for our sins when he died on the cross and rose again to save us from our punishment.[10] The Israelites rejected Jesus, but they paved the way for the Gentiles by establishing the worship of one true God on earth and bringing our Savior into this world.[11] According to the Law of Moses, Ruth was not allowed into the family of God.[1] But, there was a greater law previously established by God that overruled the Law of Moses. Paul shares in the Book of Galatians that the true children of Abraham are those who believe like Abraham and through this belief are found to be righteous children of the faith and, thus, children of God.[12]

Therefore, just as Boaz redeemed Ruth as a Gentile and as a widow into the family of God, the church was established by its acceptance of Jesus as their Savior and became a substitute until Israel can be brought back into the fold and once again become part of God's family. Just as Jesus did for the church, one day he will also do for Israel when they, too, learn they have a Son, Jesus, as their Savior.[13] All of this reminds us that God's plan includes everyone.

Ordinary People Become Extraordinary

The story of Ruth also bridges the gap in genealogy that produced the birth line to Jesus. Through God's grace, Ruth joined his family. In the eyes of the world, Boaz and Ruth were nobodies, but through their faith, kindness, love, and obedience to God, they became the parents of a son named Obed, who became the father of Jesse, and Jesse became the father of David, who became the king of Israel. What a wonderful reward to be in the birth line that produced King David, who is a direct ancestor of Mary, the mother of Jesus, the Savior of all.[14] God delivered on his promises and, in addition, gave blessings beyond measure. Can you imagine the blessing that Ruth received by being King David's great grandmother and a direct ancestor of Jesus?

Do you see what God can do with ordinary folks? Are you willing to be obedient like Ruth and Boaz and receive the blessings God has in store for you? This story reminds us that life on earth sometimes causes us to live through a period of darkness and suffering. But, if we will be faithful through the difficult times,

God will be faithful to reward us beyond what we can ever imagine. What better reward can there be than one day being joint-heirs of God with King Jesus?[15]

For Further Discussion

- Do you see how Boaz's relative missed out on God's blessing by not being willing to take Ruth? He was afraid he would lose something. Think about this example the next time you reject what God wants for you because of something you want instead. God's gift is *always* better than what we can give or take ourselves.
- Even though there was a big age difference between Ruth and Boaz, do you see the mutual respect that turned into love? Can you believe that real love comes from mutual respect rather than feelings? Name some ways Boaz showed his love for Ruth. Name some ways Ruth showed her love for Naomi. Some acts were based on feelings, but others were based on a commitment to do what was right. Are both important? Which is more important?
- Love is a *commitment*, not just a feeling. Feelings are temporary; they come and go. True love stays through the good and bad times. When you commit to marry someone, should you make a decision on feelings alone? Is it okay to have good feelings about the one you marry? What if you do not *feel* you love your spouse anymore? What can you do to make sure your marriage does *not* end in divorce?
- Does Jesus love you no matter what you are feeling? How did he show his love for you?
- Has this story of Ruth, Naomi, and Boaz given you new insight into our relationship with Jesus and our fellow human beings?

For Further Study

1. Deuteronomy 23:3—Moabites (Ruth's ancestors) were *not* allowed to be part of God's family.
2. Ephesians 2:5–9—We are saved from death by God's grace through faith; it is a gift of God. We are not saved by our good works so that no one can boast for what he did.

3. John 3:16—God so loved the world that he gave his only begotten son so that whosoever believes in him shall have everlasting life.

4. Romans 5:8—God demonstrates his love for us in that while we were still sinners, Jesus died for us.

5. Romans 11:25–26—A partial hardening has happened to Israel until the Gentile age is over. Once this time period is over, all Israel will be saved.

6. Under the Law of Moses, widows, property, and slaves could be redeemed:
   a. Deuteronomy 25:5–10—Widows may be redeemed.
   b. Leviticus 25:23–27—Property may be redeemed.
   c. Leviticus 25:47–49—A slave may be redeemed.

7. Philippians 2:5–11—Jesus left his divine nature and humbled himself to become a man and became obedient to the point of death to save us all. And then he returned to his heavenly throne where one day every knee will bow and every tongue confess that Jesus is God.

8. Hebrews 2:14, 17—Jesus became a man to take the power of death away from the devil; through his sacrificial act, he became a faithful and merciful high priest as a substitute for all people who accept his sacrifice. That is, he satisfied once and for all the law's requirement of a sacrificial lamb for the sins of the people.

9. 2 Corinthians 5:17–19—If anyone is in Christ, he is a new creation; the old has gone, the new has come. All of this is from God, who reconciled us to himself through Christ. While God was reconciling the world to himself in Christ, he did not count men's sins against them.

10. 1 Corinthians 15:1–4, 20–22—Jesus died on the cross and rose on the third day to save all who believe.

11. Romans 9:2–5; 11:1–2, 11–12, 25–26—Israel has rejected Jesus for now, which has given the Gentiles an opportunity to find him and thus preserve the faith until Israel one day returns.

12. Galatians 3:6, 16, 24–26, 29—Even so, Abraham believed God, and it was reckoned to him as righteousness. Now the promises were spoken to Abraham and to his seed. He does not say, "And to seeds," as referring to many, but to one, "And to your seed," that is, Christ. Therefore, the Law has become our tutor to lead us to Christ so that we may be justified by faith. But now that faith has come, we are no longer under a tutor. For you are all sons of God through faith in Christ Jesus. And if you belong to Christ, then you are Abraham's descendants and heirs according to God's promise.

13. Romans 11:25–26—Israel will return to God and will be saved when the fullness of the Gentiles has come.

14. The genealogy provided in the New Testament: First, the Gospel of Matthew gives the King's birth line through Joseph, which supports Jesus' earthly right to be King as the adopted son of Joseph. And then the Gospel of Luke gives the King's birth line through Mary, which supports the virgin birth and Jesus' heavenly right to be King. [Note: Luke says the "supposed" son of Joseph; thus, many Bible scholars believe this means Luke's genealogy is Mary's birth line as the names are the same from Abraham to David but change with the son of David. In Luke the son of David listed is Nathan (not Solomon), the line of David through whom Mary was born.]

    a. Matthew 1:1–16—The line of Jesus through Joseph, David, and Boaz and Ruth

    b. Luke 3:23–38—The line of Jesus through Mary, David, and Boaz

15. Romans 8:16–17—As children of God, which we become through believing and receiving Jesus, we are heirs of God and fellow heirs with Jesus.

Chapter 13

JOB, A MAN PLEASING TO GOD: PART 1
Job 1–42

The Bible tells of Job, a man of God, blameless and upright. We know very little about his family history, and we do not know the names of his children or his descendants; we don't even know if he was an Israelite. The story is not found in the historical books of the Old Testament. Instead, the Book of Job is the first book in the Poetry and Wisdom section of the Bible, which includes with Psalms and Proverbs. We are not even sure at what point in history Job lived. Even though Job is not among the historical books, I believe this is a true story that provides wonderful insights into heaven—specifically, what goes on before the throne of God.

Job lived either while the Israelites were becoming a nation in Egypt or during the period of the judges before the kings of Israel came into power. Because he lived well beyond one hundred years, it was more likely soon after the time of Jacob and Joseph.

Job, a Blameless and Upright Man of God

Job had seven sons and three daughters and was very rich. God blessed him greatly with seven thousand sheep, three thousand camels, five hundred oxen, and five hundred female donkeys; in addition, he had many servants to take care of his animals and possessions. He was well-known as the greatest man in the East.

More important, Job was blameless and upright, fearing God and turning away from evil. Wouldn't you love to hear God say such wonderful things about you? Each time I fail to serve God in the way I know he wants me to, I think of Job or one of the other characters in the Bible of whom God speaks highly. Instead of feeling bad, I repent and strive to be more like these examples as I know God is merciful to forgive me. And he will do the same for you.

Job's sons often had parties, and during these times of celebration, the brothers took turns hosting each other and their sisters. Each brother took a day of the week to provide food and entertainment. Job worried that with so much celebration, surely, they had done things that were not pleasing to God. He feared they may have even cursed God in their hearts. To compensate, he offered sacrifices to God on their behalf. I have heard some share a belief that Job's fear about his children led to some of his problems. I do not believe that was it as all loving parents should be concerned for their children. Offering sacrifices was a form of prayer in these Old Testament times. I have learned from Job to dedicate specific times to pray for my children.

Praying for Our Families

A group of men from my Sunday school class meets each Monday to pray for our children and grandchildren for many of the same reasons Job did. When we know of a specific need, we ask for God's help, but our primary motive is to lift our family up to God, praying for each to have a closer walk with Jesus. We have seen God answer many of our prayers, and we continue to have needs that we lift up to God.

I share this to encourage you to consider establishing a time to pray for your family. Further, it helps to have a small group of close friends with whom you can share confidential and personal family details. My mother once said something that I have always remembered. She told my wife and me that she promised not to get upset when we did not take her advice *if* we promised not to get mad when she offered it. Parents have a hard time *not* offering advice. So, this may be a good compromise for all of us. However, I have learned that I may not be the one to solve my children's problems. They may not always need my help, and, for sure, they do not always want it. Accordingly, our group is learning that our prayers are more effective than our advice, and we are learning *not* to give advice unless it is asked for—or at least refrain more often than we used to. I suggest the same for you.

The Battle on the Heavenly Front

Moving back to the story of Job, we notice a dramatic shift in scene. We are given a bird's-eye view of what was going on in heaven while Job lived his life on earth. There was a day when the angels came to present themselves before God, and Satan (the devil) also came. Consider this astounding and very revealing exchange between God and Satan:

God said to Satan, "From where do you come?"

Satan answered, "From roaming about the earth."

"Have you considered my servant Job?" God asked. "For there is no one like him on earth, a blameless and upright man, fearing God and turning away from evil."

"Does Job fear God for nothing?" Satan answered. "Have you not made a hedge about him and his house? You have blessed the work of his hands and have increased his possessions greatly. I say put forth your hand and cause him to lose all of his possessions, and he will curse you."

The Lord said, "Behold all that he has is in your power; only do not put forth your hand on him."

So, Satan departed from the presence of God.

What a remarkable exchange! We know from earlier stories in the Old Testament that God and Satan are enemies. This scene takes place after Satan's failed attempt to take God's throne. Satan is not only allowed to enter the presence of God but is also allowed to challenge him. It would appear that Satan is tricking God and maybe even deceiving him. But if we think that, we fail in understanding our all-knowing God. For just as God had an ulterior motive in allowing Jesus to be crucified through the betrayal of Judas, whom Satan had entered,[1] God would also make sure that what Satan meant for evil would turn into good for Job. We need to remember that Jesus was called to suffer, and as his disciples, we, too, may be called to suffer in this life.[2] We will see that Job suffered through a very difficult period. I think Job's story is presented to help us get through difficulties in our lives, to help us trust that God has a plan—even when we cannot see the end result.

The Battle from the Earthly Perspective

Satan believed Job was serving God because God protected him from harm and blessed him in so many ways. God was willing to test Satan's theory, and Job was truly put through the wringer:

First, a messenger came to tell Job that the Sabeans attacked his servants, taking all of the oxen and donkeys; they slew all of the servants except this one man who escaped to tell Job the news.

While the servant was still speaking, another servant came and said,

"The fire of God fell from heaven and burned up the sheep and servants, and I alone have escaped to tell you."

While the servant was still speaking, another servant came and said,

"The Chaldeans made a raid on your camels and took them, killing all of your servants, and I alone have escaped to tell you."

While the servant was still speaking, another servant came and said,

"Your sons and daughters were eating and drinking wine in the oldest brother's house, and a great wind came forth and crushed the house, killing all of your children and servants, and I alone have escaped to tell you."

Can you comprehend the devastation and grief Job experienced all at once? Imagine learning that you lost all of your material possessions, followed by the news that all of your children have been killed by a storm—particularly traumatic news for Job after all of his prayers for them. He was not aware that this attack came directly from Satan. Much of this assault appeared to be from his human enemies, but we know better. When Satan hits, he often hits hard. So, when you are attacked, remember this story and be careful who you blame for your difficulties. However, while we need to be aware of Satan's presence and his desire to cause us harm, I do not think we should automatically think it is Satan that has caused the problem. But as we see from this story, he is a powerful enemy that we need to acknowledge and be prepared for.

Job arose and tore his robe and shaved his head, both signs of humility and grief. Then he fell to the ground and worshipped God. What? He worshipped God. You would think he would have been crying out in anger, but no. Instead, he worshipped God and said,

> *Naked I came from my mother's womb and naked I shall return. The Lord gave, and the Lord has taken away. Blessed be the name of the Lord.*

In spite of the devastating losses, Job did not sin, nor did he blame God. Could you find that kind of strength in your faith?

Back in Heaven

Again, there was a day when the angels came to present themselves before God, and again, Satan was there. A similar exchange took place:

> *God said to Satan, "From where do you come?"*

> *Satan answered, "From roaming about the earth."*

> *"Have you considered my servant Job? For there is no one like him on earth, a blameless and upright man, fearing God and turning away from evil. [But this time God adds,] He still holds fast his integrity, although you incited me to ruin him without cause."*

[Note: God was not the one who caused the harm, but he did give permission to Satan.]

> *Satan replied, "Skin for skin! Yes, all that a man has he will give for his life. Allow me to harm his flesh and bones, and he will curse you."*

> *So, the Lord said, "Behold, he is in your power, only spare his life."*

This exchange clearly shows a battle in the heavenly or spiritual realm, a world we cannot see. We first talked about this realm in Volume 1 of this series, in the "Tower of Babel" story. This spiritual world is in its own dimension, and we only have access to it when God, or perhaps at times Satan, allows us a window from which we may view it. Through the picture we see in this story, we gain a better understanding of God's world and our access to it in a time of need.

Because we only get such a small glimpse into what takes place in heaven, it may seem that Job is like a toy that God and Satan are fighting over. It is *not* true that we are like pawns or that God chooses to play with us in any cruel manner he pleases. *But it is true* that we are foot soldiers in a battle in which God asks us to do things that may not make sense to us.[3]

Consider past wars. During World War II, many soldiers died on the battlefield when they crossed the English Channel on D-Day, June 6, 1944. It did not seem fair that these soldiers had to die, but it was necessary to win the war. For without the successful crossing into France, the Allied forces would not have been able to defeat Hitler and the German army. Most of the soldiers did not fully understand what they were being asked to do. Nevertheless, they did understand they might sacrifice their own lives for their country. In spite of great peril, in faith, they followed orders.

The few were sacrificed for the many. When we fight in God's army, we may not understand all that he asks us to do. But if we will trust him, one day we will understand the danger, the difficulties, and, yes, even the pain that was necessary to achieve his ultimate plan. He is preparing a place for each of us in eternity with him, where we will enjoy the fruits of our labor, the special rewards waiting for those who suffer for Jesus.[4] Until then, we need to acknowledge the scripture verse in Ephesians where we are encouraged,

> *Finally, be strong in the Lord and in the strength of his might. Put on the full armor of God so that you may be able to stand firm against the schemes of the devil. For our struggle is not against flesh and blood, but . . . against the spiritual forces of wickedness in the heavenly places.*[5]

We must accept the challenge to be in God's army and help him fight the enemy. Are you ready at any cost? If so, look to that day when God will say to you,

> *Well done, my good and faithful servant . . . Enter into the joy of the Lord.*[6]

Back to the Battleground

Well, Job was now being put to the test even further. He may not have completely understood that he was a soldier of God, but it would not be long before he found out. This is why we need to learn the lesson and be prepared for the attack of the enemy.

Satan was allowed to inflict pain and disease upon him. And so he did. Satan left the presence of God and struck Job with sore boils from the sole of his foot to the crown of his head. Job was in extreme pain and misery, so much so that his wife declared,

Do you still hold fast your integrity? Curse God and die!

Now listen to Job's reply, even in the midst of his excruciating pain:

You speak as one of the foolish women. Shall we indeed accept good from God and not accept adversity?

I am truly amazed at the faith of this man, Job. Could you stand firm in the face of such pain and agony? I personally know two people who did: a man of God named Bill, who is now with Jesus, and a godly woman named Brooke. I admire them greatly. Do you know someone of whom you can say the same thing? Hold fast to God's truth, and you will see the glory of the Lord. The only way to endure is to remember that we will have victory with Jesus.

Satan now leaves the picture, and we do not hear from him again. He lost the battle with God, but our story is far from over. Job must still contend with the devastation left by Satan's attacks. He continued to experience intense suffering caused by the boils all over his body and the painful memory of the death of his children.

For Further Discussion

- Do you understand the importance of prayer? Have you prayed enough to know that it works? Does it help to be blameless before God like Job was?
- Why do you think God let Satan attack Job and his family?
- What was the purpose of Job's suffering? Is it okay if we don't fully know?
- How do you intend to handle suffering when you are not aware of anything you did wrong? Is it okay to ask for the suffering to be removed?
- What did you learn from this story about the spiritual world? How do you get there?
- Explain Job's continual faith in God in spite of all the attacks.

For Further Study

1. Luke 22:2–6—The Jewish leaders were looking for someone to help them arrest Jesus. Judas, one of the twelve, agreed to be the one when he allowed Satan to enter his body.
2. 1 Peter 4:1–2, 12–14—Jesus suffered when he sacrificed himself for each of us. We, in turn, may be called upon to suffer when others persecute us because we stand up for him.
3. 2 Timothy 2:3–4—We are soldiers of Christ in active service, and we need to pay attention to our duties, rather than the everyday affairs of this world.
4. 1 Corinthians 3:10–14—Our actions and deeds will be put to the test of fire when we stand before God. Those that endure the fire will result in a reward for believers.
5. Ephesians 6:10–12—We must be ready to stand firm against the devil and his evil angels in the heavenly realm (spiritual world).
6. Matthew 25:21—When we live our lives by serving God, we can look forward to God receiving us into heaven as faithful servants.

Chapter 14
JOB, A MAN PLEASING TO GOD: PART 2
Job 1–42

We learned in part 1 of Job's story that he was a man of God, blameless and upright. But he was suffering greatly from a disease Satan brought on his entire body. In addition to the physical pain Job was enduring, he lost all of his immense fortune and suffered through the death of all ten of his children in one day. All of this misfortune and grief was caused by Satan in his direct attempt to challenge God. To this point, Job had maintained his faith and trust in God. It is impossible to grasp how very difficult this must have been.

Friends Come to Offer Support but Then Criticize

Upon hearing of Job's misfortune, three friends came to comfort and sympathize with him. As they approached, they did not recognize him. They cried loudly and wept inconsolably for him. For seven days and seven nights, they sat beside him in complete silence, for they saw how great his pain was.

The pain continued so long that Job finally opened his mouth and cursed the day of his birth. He longed for death and exclaimed, "For what I fear comes upon me, and what I dread befalls me." He could not stand the pain any longer and lost his cool for a time. I think we can all empathize with Job. There was no relief in sight, and he questioned why this happened to him. He did not blame God, but he could not understand what he had done to deserve such punishment. He examined himself thoroughly and concluded he had done nothing to warrant this.

His friends, Eliphaz, Bildad, and Zophar, thought they had the answers. I am not sure why they transitioned from sympathizing and crying with him to criticizing him, but I guess that is what friends will do. The next twenty-eight

115

chapters of the Book of Job detail the conversations between Job and his three friends. Each friend gave his opinion about what Job had done wrong to bring on this calamity and also argued with him. In essence, they told Job that he deserved this and insisted that if he would just repent and ask God for forgiveness, all would be right and he would be healed. Job strongly disagreed and hotly protested their points. He was adamant that he had done nothing for which he needed to ask forgiveness, and he would not let them intimidate him into saying he had. What began as sympathy for Job concluded in an intense argument with no resolution.

Can you recall a time where you tried to help a friend, but the friend simply would not listen? Or maybe someone tried to tell you that you were wrong when you knew very well that you were not. How sad that we turn on each other! I pray we will learn to share what we think about certain situations without turning on friends, fellow church members, or co-workers, as that behavior will not end with a positive result.[1] How can we learn to work and live together with our fellow human beings?

Consensus Building

Building a consensus is one of the best ways to reach agreement on a difficult matter. The following is a good example of what I mean by this. In 1984, four fellow CPAs and I formed a new accounting firm. All five of us had strong opinions and diverse personalities. But our differences became a strength for our firm.

When we had different ideas on how to handle a matter, we came together to discuss the issue. We generally came away with a sound conclusion (a consensus) because each of us was determined to make the decision that was best for the firm, instead of what was best for us individually.

Church meetings often end with hard feelings because of diverse viewpoints. Countless churches split over minor differences—although I am sure the people involved did not believe that the disagreements were minor. Some of the disputes may have been important, but more often than not, we should be able to work through opposing opinions. For example, several years ago, our church was going through some difficult financial times, and we needed to vote on major cuts in the budget. While the vote did not specifically say that certain staff positions would be eliminated, everyone knew that this would be the next step.

The vote ended up eighteen for the cuts and fifteen against. No one felt good about it; the vote was too close, and we were *not* a unified body. I suggested we table the issue and revisit the matter another time when we might reach a better decision. Interestingly enough, *everyone* agreed. We later came back and agreed on another path. It still was a tough decision because the money was not there, but it was a decision that the consensus now believed was the right one.

I believe families, churches, and businesses can learn from these examples. When varying opinions are presented, the desire to make the *right* decision needs to be the focal point—not what *you* believe to be right. We will not all agree on how to approach a problem or decision. God made each of us unique so that we can help one another see all sides to a situation. Instead of fighting the differences, let's learn to listen and be open for the Holy Spirit to guide us into all truths.[2]

A New Face and a New Perspective Enters the Picture

In Job chapter 32, we learn there was a fourth person who accompanied Job's friends. He was a young man named Elihu. Out of respect for his elders, he kept quiet during all of the discussions.[3] But when Job and the three friends became silent, Elihu spoke up. His anger burned against Job because he (Job) justified himself before God; he was also angry with his friends because they found no answer, yet condemned Job.

While at first Elihu was respectful of his elders, he believed he had the answer. He waited to hear the right answer, but none came. He told Job that he had no right to question God's actions or decisions. He was quite eloquent in his speech, but also very direct, as shown in the following excerpt:

Behold, I belong to God like you; I, too, have been formed out of clay. No fear of me should terrify you, nor should my pressure weigh heavily on you. But here's what I heard you say, Job: "I am pure, without transgression; I am innocent and there is no guilt in me." Behold, let me tell you, you are not right in this, for God is greater than man. Why do you complain against him that he did not give an account of all of his doings? God speaks, but yet no one notices it.

[Let a man get into trouble], then he will pray to God, and God will accept him that he may restore his righteousness to man . . . For God oftentimes brings back man's soul from the grave, that he may be enlightened.

Pay attention, Job, listen to me; keep silent, and let me speak; then if you have something to say, answer me. Speak, for I desire to justify you. If not, keep silent, and I will teach you wisdom.

What powerful and prophetic words from a much younger man, although his concluding words may have crossed the line to inappropriate—especially in these Old Testament times where the elders spoke, and the younger men were expected to be silent and listen. In this case, Elihu felt he had heard enough; he heard no wisdom and felt he had powerful words from God. He condemned the three friends. He told them, "Far be it from God to do wickedness . . . nor will he pervert justice." He went on to say much more, but in summary, he told them that none of them, including Job, had the right to question God and they all spoke without knowledge. The basis of his words was true. However, interestingly enough, we will see that God did not give him credit for any of his speech. I believe God did not like his disrespectful and arrogant attitude.

God Enters and Takes Charge

After Elihu finally finished speaking, God answered Job and ignored the words of any of the others, including Elihu. Here are a few of the words God contemptuously spoke to Job:

> *Who is this that darkens counsel by words without knowledge? Now gird up your loins like a man, and I'll ask you and you instruct me! Where were you when I laid the foundations of the earth? Tell me, if you have understanding.*

> *Since you know, when did the morning stars sing together and all the angels shout for joy? Have you ever in your life commanded the morning and caused the dawn to know its place?*

> *Can you hunt the prey for the lion? Or satisfy the appetite of the young lions? Is it by your understanding that the hawk soars, stretching his wings toward the South? Is it at your command that the eagle mounts up and makes his nest on high?*

> *God went on to say, "Will the faultfinder contend with the Almighty? Let him who reproves God answer it."*

> *Job wisely answered, "Behold, I am insignificant; what can I reply to you? I place my hand on my mouth. Once I have spoken, I will not answer even twice; I will say no more."*

> *God continued to criticize Job, "I will ask you, and you instruct me. Will you really annul my judgment? Will you really condemn me that you may be justified? [You be God and] pour out the overflowing of your anger and look on everyone who is proud to make him low."*

Finally, Job is given the opportunity to repent, and he does so graciously and thankfully:

I know that you can do all things and that no purpose of yours can be thwarted. Hear now, and I will speak; I will ask you, and you instruct me . . . Therefore, I retract, and I repent in dust and ashes.

After Job repented, God turned to Eliphaz and said,

My wrath is kindled against you and against your friends because you have not spoken what is right as my servant Job has. Now, therefore, take seven bulls and seven rams and present them as a burnt offering; afterwards, my servant Job will pray for you. I will accept his offering so that I may not do with you according to your folly.

So, Eliphaz, Bildad, and Zophar did as the Lord instructed them, and God accepted Job's prayer for these men. I want you to notice that God was silent in regard to Elihu. He did not criticize him, nor did he give him credit for his words of wisdom. His words were right, although some of his words were spoken disrespectfully.

It is interesting to note that God was complimentary of Job when he spoke to Eliphaz. While God was upset with Job, he understood that Job never lost his faith in him. While he was frustrated and even criticized God, Job maintained his trust in God, whom he loved. Once he repented, God was ready to forgive Job. He was even ready to forgive Job's friends for their foolish words and for not realizing that Job was "blameless, upright, fearing God, and turning away from evil."

What a great lesson for us to learn: God is in control. While we may not understand all that is going on around us, we must let God stay in charge and follow the course he has laid out for us. That does not mean we cannot cry out for help or even question why. But when we do not get an answer or do not get the answer we want, let's be faithful to serve God and continue on the path laid out for us.[4]

God Restores All and More to Job

After Job prayed for God to forgive his friends, God was ready to heal Job and restore all that he lost. He not only restored to Job all that was his before but gave him twice as much: seven thousand sheep became fourteen thousand, three thousand camels became six thousand, and five hundred oxen and female donkeys became one thousand each. And God blessed Job and his wife with seven sons and three daughters. Notice that Job received double of all that he had, except for his children. Why not twice as many children? My belief is that his children who died earlier were in heaven, so he did receive double of all he had before.

It is interesting that the Bible gave the names of his three daughters and noted that no women in all the land were as beautiful as his daughters. Even more interesting, his daughters were given an inheritance equal to their brothers, which was contrary to the practice in which the sons generally received the entire inheritance. I believe there is a message here that God is confirming women are equally blessed in his kingdom.[5]

Job lived one hundred forty years longer to enjoy four generations of his family. So, although he suffered dearly for a time, through no fault of his own, he died an old man, full of days.

Job's suffering must have been for a greater good. Perhaps it was for growth in his own character or to demonstrate the sovereignty of God or simply for the fulfillment of God's master plans. Job became a victim of the spiritual warfare that takes place every day, much like many soldiers of Christ who suffer in Jesus' name. Job was unaware of the battle that took place between God and Satan behind the scenes. We, too, may be unaware of the circumstances that result in troubling events in our lives, but we are called to be faithful and trust that God has our best interest at heart in all he allows.[6]

For Further Discussion

- How do you think you should approach people who are suffering? What would you say differently if you thought it was because of something they had done wrong? What if it did not look as if they had done anything wrong? Could it be God's fault? Should the suffering person blame God?
- Have you ever had friends turn against you but were not sure why? Is it possible they thought they were helping you?
- Do you see the value in consensus building rather than simply going with the majority?
- What did Elihu say that was right? Do you think he said anything inappropriate?
- How would you have felt if God had spoken to you like he did to Job? To Job's friends?
- Was Job a better person as a result of all he went through? Did he learn a lesson?

- We face many things in life that are hard to accept and understand. Often, God is ready to step in and help us immediately. Other times, God wants us to learn a valuable lesson from the difficult circumstances, so he may delay in giving his help. Are you ready to look for the lesson and learn from it when this happens to you?

For Further Study

1. Ephesians 4:1–3, 16—We are called to work together as one common body, showing partiality to each other with everyone doing their part.
2. John 16:13—The Holy Spirit has been given to us to receive messages from God and guide us into all truths.
3. 1 Timothy 5:1–2—Men and women both are called to respect their elders.
4. James 1:2–4—Consider it all joy, my brethren, when you encounter various trials, knowing that the testing of your faith produces endurance. And let endurance have its perfect result so that you may be perfect and complete, lacking in nothing.
5. Galatians 3:27–28—In Christ, all are equal, including male and female.
6. Romans 8:38–39—For I am sure that neither death nor life, nor angels nor rulers, nor things present nor things to come, nor powers, nor height nor depth, nor anything else in all creation will be able to separate us from the love of God through Jesus.

Chapter 15
AN ANOINTED JUDGE AND PROPHET
I Samuel 1–16

As you read the first few paragraphs of this story, consider who the person may be. You may be able to guess; however, there is an interesting twist.

Preparing the Way for the King

Once there was a couple who wanted to have a child very much; however, even though they had been married a long time, they were never able to have children. So, they prayed and asked God to send them a son. They promised God that if he would answer their prayer, they would dedicate their son to God to be a Nazirite. You may remember from the story of Samson that a Nazirite is someone dedicated to God who agrees not to drink wine nor cut his hair. In this case, the son's life would be dedicated to serving God, much like our preachers today but with a very specific purpose to be carried out for God.

One day, God answered the couple's prayer by sending his messenger to share the good news that a son was on the way. He was indeed a special son. Not only did he spend his entire life faithfully serving God, but he also prepared the way for the coming king for God's people, and he called the people to repentance. Many listened to his voice and repented of their sins.

Near the end of his life, this man was called to anoint a very special person. As he anointed him, the Spirit of God descended upon him, and God announced this person would be on the throne of his kingdom.

I am sure many of you have heard this story and by now have guessed this Nazirite was John the Baptist. But the twist I promised you is that this could just as easily be the story of Samuel, a judge and a prophet who later in life anointed David as king of Israel. Isn't it interesting how the Bible teaches us about two men who were both very special to God whose lives and purpose were very much the same? Let's look more carefully at the lives of Samuel and John the Baptist. We will find that Samuel was not only a person assigned to prepare the way for David, the king of Israel, but he was also a picture of John the Baptist, who would one day prepare the way for the coming of King Jesus.

Throughout the Old Testament, we find that God gave us pictures of Jesus and God's plan for mankind. In this Old Testament story, we are given a prophecy (God's plan revealed) that he would send a forerunner (Samuel as a portrait of John the Baptist) to prepare the way for the coming of our eternal king (David as a picture of Jesus). While not everything about the two men is alike, a remarkable comparison clearly exists.

Below is a list that identifies the many similarities of the lives of these two men.

In regard to their parents:

- Both couples were righteous before God, but neither had been able to have a child for many years.[1a]
- Each wife felt it was a disgrace to be unable to have children.[1b]
- Both couples made a special prayer request for a child, which God delivered.[1c]
- Both couples were told that their sons were to carry out special plans given by God.[1d]

In regard to Samuel and John the Baptist:

- Both were lifetime Nazirites.[2a]
- Samuel was the last judge before King David and the first prophet. John was the last prophet before Jesus (the King of Kings) and John was the first believer of Jesus.[2b]
- Both were called to prepare the way (to act as a forerunner) for the coming king (David/Jesus).[2c]
- Both lived during a time when Israel was not following God.[2d]
- Both were great men of God.[2e]
- Both called Israel to repentance.[2f]
- Both anointed the king of Israel (David/Jesus).[2g]
- As both were anointed (David/Jesus), the Holy Spirit came upon the future king.[2h]
- Both fade into the background after the anointing of the king.[2i]

After having revealed so many similarities, is there any doubt that God is showing us through the life of Samuel that he had planned well beforehand that John the Baptist would prepare the way for Jesus, which further builds evidence that Jesus is who he said he is?

Birth of Samuel

Let's look more closely at Samuel's birth and life story.

Elkanah lived in the country of Israel with his two wives, Hannah and Penninah. Penninah had many children while Hannah had none. Every year, Elkanah would go to Shiloh to offer a sacrifice to the Lord and thank him for all the blessings God bestowed unto him. He always offered a special sacrifice for Penninah for all the children she bore him, and because he loved Hannah so much, he always gave a double portion for her, even though she had no children.

Hannah was distraught because she was unable to bear children. It was very important to women in Old Testament times to have children because they were judged by their friends based on how many sons they gave birth to;[3] therefore, it was viewed as a disgrace not to have at least one son. To make matters worse, each year as they went for the special sacrifice, Penninah would tease Hannah so badly that she would weep and not eat. Elkanah would try to comfort her, "Isn't my love better than ten sons?" But this never satisfied Hannah.

One year Hannah was determined to pray before the Lord at the time of the sacrifice. As she approached the altar, Hannah humbly bowed and very intently prayed, begging God for a son. She promised God that if he would give her a son, she would dedicate him to the Lord; and further, he would drink no wine nor cut his hair, thus following the Jewish custom for setting someone apart as a Nazirite, a person dedicated to serve the Lord in a special way. Similarly, today we have monks and nuns who have chosen to dedicate their entire lives to God.

Hannah was praying so hard and weeping so much that Eli, the chief priest and judge of Israel at this time, came over to see what was wrong. As he approached her, he believed she was drunk and scolded her for coming into God's presence in such a state. Hannah explained that she was not drunk and confessed the reason for her extreme sorrow.

After hearing from God, Eli promised her that by the following year she would have a child. Hannah went home rejoicing, her face no longer sad because she had received a promise from God. Less than a year later, Hannah gave birth to a son. She celebrated, saying, "Because I have asked for him from the Lord, I shall call him Samuel."

We, too, can go before the Lord with our needs, but like Hannah, we may have to humble ourselves and even plead with God to honor our request. Sometimes what we think we need and want is not really what is best according to God's bigger plan. At the right time—his right time—God will always meet our true needs (based on *his* definition of needs, not ours) and honorable wants. As children, our fathers make decisions for us when we are not old enough to understand; accordingly, we must have faith in God that he is taking care of us, as a true father, and accept his decisions. We must trust that God is faithful, and, at times, we have to be willing to persevere and wait on his timing.[4]

Dedication of Samuel

When Elkanah took his family to the annual sacrifice the following year, Hannah did not go because Samuel was just a baby. She told Elkanah that she planned to dedicate Samuel to the Lord and would give her son to Eli so he could grow up as a priest under Eli's apprenticeship. When Samuel was old enough, Hannah made a special trip to visit Eli and presented Samuel to him, saying, "I am the woman who stood beside you praying to the Lord for this boy. I prayed, and the Lord has given me my desire. So, now I am honoring my promise to the Lord. I give Samuel to you to be trained as a priest." Eli worshipped God and thanked him for this special son, Samuel. Then Hannah offered a special prayer to the Lord:

> *My heart is happy. My cup is filled with joy because the Lord has answered my prayer. There is no one holy like the Lord. Indeed, there is no other God but you. The mighty Lord will defeat all of our enemies and those who are hungry will be fed by the Lord; even those women who have no children can have children because the Lord grants their requests.*

Hannah was sending each of us a message: God can answer all of our troubles and will meet all of our needs. He is there when we need him. He will provide salvation, and he sent his Son to die for us so that we may live with him forever. Are we willing to listen to these prophetic words of Hannah? If we do,

our lives will change. We will no longer be anxious when things are not going the way we expect or want; instead, we will be ready to call upon the Lord. And we will be ready for his call to us.

We will learn in later stories how Samuel was called for a special purpose, to call God's family to repentance and prepare the way for King David—just as John the Baptist did one thousand years later. As we discussed earlier in this story, he, too, called the people to repentance and prepared the way for King Jesus.

For Further Discussion

- Why do you think God chose to give us prophecies of John the Baptist and his plans for us through this Old Testament story?
- Does it help you understand and accept God's plan for your life when you see his plans for others revealed through these stories?
- Have you ever wanted something so much that you committed to lay your need before God in such a way that God knew you were serious about getting an answer from him?
- Repentance was the message of both Samuel and John the Baptist; they came to show us the way to Jesus. Are you listening?

For Further Study

1. Scriptures comparing the events behind the birth of Samuel with the birth of John the Baptist:
   a. 1 Samuel 1:3–5, 9–11; Luke 1:5–7
   b. Genesis 30: 22–23; 1 Samuel 1:11; Luke 1:25
   c. 1 Samuel 1:4–5; 11–18; Luke 1:11–13
   d. 1 Samuel 1:20–22, 27–28; Luke 1:14–16
2. Scriptures comparing the life of Samuel with the life of John the Baptist:
   a. Numbers 6:1–21; 1 Samuel 1:11; Luke 1:15
   b. 1 Samuel 3:20; 7:15–17; 8:4–7,19–22; Luke 3:4–6; Matthew 3:11; 11:12–13
   c. 1 Samuel 16:1,12–13; Luke 1:17
   d. 1 Samuel 3:1; Luke 1:16; 3:2–3,7–8
   e. 1 Samuel 3:19–21; 7:15–17; Matthew 11:11
   f. 1 Samuel 7:3–5; Matthew 3:1–2
   g. 1 Samuel 16:1,11–13; Matthew 3:13–17
   h. 1 Samuel 16:13; Matthew 3:16
   i. 1 Samuel 12:1–4; John 3:28–31
3. Other examples of women who, for a time, had no children:
   a. Genesis 15:1–4; 16:1–2; 18:9–14—The agony of Abraham and Sarah because they had no children; note God's promises to deliver in his time.
   b. Genesis 25:21—And Isaac prayed to the Lord for his wife because she was barren. And the Lord granted his prayer, and Rebekah, his wife, conceived.
   c. Genesis 29:31; 30:1—When the Lord saw that Leah was hated, he opened her womb, but Rachel was barren. When Rachel saw that she bore Jacob no children, she envied her sister. She said to Jacob, "Give me children, or I shall die!"
   d. Deuteronomy 7:14—You shall be blessed above all peoples. There shall not be male or female barren among you or among your livestock.
4. James 1:12—Blessed is the one who perseveres under trial because, having stood the test, that person will receive the crown of life that the Lord has promised to those who love him.

Chapter 16

GOD'S CALL TO SAMUEL

1 Samuel 2–3

When we left Samuel in the last story, his mother, Hannah, had dedicated him to the Lord by sending him to Eli, the chief priest, for training in the priesthood. She did so to honor the promise she made to God when he fulfilled her request for a long-awaited son. Eli was also a judge in Israel who served God faithfully; he told Hannah God would grant her a son. Samuel grew up in Eli's home and was pleasing to the Lord. For her faithfulness to God, he granted Hannah more children. She visited Samuel regularly, and each year, she made him a new Ephod suit (a priestly robe like the adults wore when they served God). Even at a young age, Samuel understood the things of

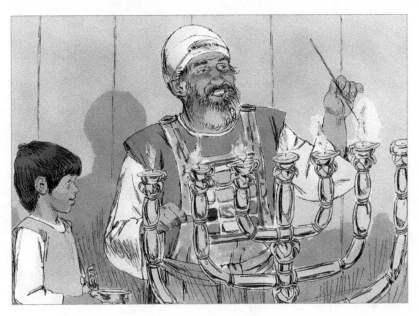

God, and all those around him knew he was special and would one day be a leader of God's people.

Once Again, Trouble in Israel

Meanwhile, as Eli retired from some of his priestly duties, the people complained to him that his sons, Hophni and Phinehas, were taking advantage of their roles as priests in the house of Israel. As good as Eli was, he would not properly discipline his sons. As a result, God proclaimed that Eli's descendants would be "cut off" from the priesthood. Today, many parents are like Eli; they may be good people, but they have blind spots when it comes to their children. Parents will not accept that their children behave badly and need to be corrected or punished.

The Book of Hebrews says that if you are without discipline, you are not sons; rather, you are illegitimate children. In the same way that parents discipline their children, God disciplines us because he loves us, and we need his guidance and corrective action, which allows us to share in his holiness.[1] So we are out of sync with God's expectation when we do not properly discipline our own children.

With Eli's sons shirking their priestly responsibilities, God was preparing Samuel to take their place. We have previously discussed how Aaron's family from the tribe of Levi was given the privilege to be the high priests for God's Chosen People. Remember, the priests were similar to our preachers. However, in those days, people did not have direct access to God like we do today. Hebrew priests were the direct communication link to God. The people would take their request to the priests, who would relay their prayer to God as Eli had done for Hannah. The priests also offered many sacrifices on a continual basis, asking for forgiveness for the many sins of the people. Samuel was given the privilege of serving as a high priest, even though he was not a descendant of Aaron.

God Calls

One night while Samuel was still a young boy, he heard a voice call out his name. He jumped up from his bed and ran to Eli and asked, "Did you call me? What do you want?" Eli responded to Samuel, saying, "I did not call you, Samuel. Go back to bed." After Samuel returned to bed, he heard the call again, "Samuel, Samuel." Again, he jumped up and responded to Eli, saying, "Eli, sir, what is it that you wish me to do?" Eli again told him, "You must have been dreaming. Go back to bed." A third time the Lord called to Samuel, but this time, Eli realized that God was calling Samuel, so he told him to listen for the voice of God and to respond, "Here I am, Lord. What is it that you wish of me?"

Visions from God were very rare in those days because the people were not pleasing to God. Even though Samuel grew up in Eli's presence, he did not know God spoke directly to his people. But when the Lord called Samuel the fourth time, he followed Eli's instructions and responded, "Speak, for I am your servant;

I am listening." The Lord told Samuel that he (God) was ready to carry out the punishment for Eli's sons and end Eli's ministry.

Many people believe God does not speak to us like this today. However, I truly believe that we, too, can hear from God. Maybe we do not hear because we, like the people in Samuel's day, are not pleasing to God. Maybe it is because we do not set aside time for God. We need to be quiet and listen, but God does not necessarily speak when we want him to. God, through his son, Jesus, will speak when he is ready. We need to know Jesus well enough to recognize his voice when he does speak. This requires time in prayer and meditation. In the Gospel of John, Jesus tells his followers that he is the good shepherd; he knows his flock and his flock knows him. His sheep hear his voice and follow. [2]

We Are the Sheep and Jesus Is Our Shepherd

Beginning with Abraham, God's Chosen People have been shepherds. The people of Samuel's time would have understood the important lesson we can learn from the relationship between a shepherd and his sheep. Sheep learn to trust their shepherd and follow his voice. The shepherd can put his sheep in a fence with other sheep and never get them mixed up, even though they are not branded. When the shepherd comes to get his sheep, he can call and his sheep will follow. [3]

However, sheep are not smart animals. So, it is important that they have masters (shepherds) who will care for them. I have heard that sheep will follow the voice of their shepherd wherever he leads them—even if he leads them to walk off a cliff. One by one, the sheep will plunge, not realizing they are falling to their death. This seems crazy, but in many ways, we are no better. Jesus pleads with us to follow him and ignore the voice of the devil. However, we are too much like the sheep. Unfortunately, too often we have learned to recognize the voice of this world (the devil), and thus, follow the voice of the wrong shepherd.

The devil's voice can be enticing; his way sounds so good and seems like so much fun. But Jesus warns us: the devil comes to kill, steal, and destroy. [4] Like the sheep, we can easily fall off the cliff. Too often, we believe the ways of this world (the devil's world) are the right way. Like Samuel, we as Christians must take time to learn Jesus' voice so that we, like sheep, can know and follow our true shepherd's call. One of the best ways to learn our shepherd's voice is to study and know the Bible – God's Word. I encourage you to take time daily to absorb what God is saying to you in his Word through time spent meditating and communicating with Jesus.

Are You Prepared?

Now, back to God's message to Samuel. When morning came, Samuel was afraid to tell Eli the word God shared with him because he knew how upset Eli would be. However, Eli pressed Samuel to tell him exactly what God said without hiding anything. Therefore, Samuel told Eli what God thought about his sons and how they would die. Eli sadly accepted their fate. While we often have to accept the consequences of our actions, it is nice to know that God forgives those who believe in him.[5] Would you rather be like Samuel or like Eli's sons, Hophni and Phinehas? Both grew up under Eli, a godly priest, but each had his own choice to make. Samuel chose to listen to the voice of God, but Hophni and Phinehas chose to listen to the voice of evil. In the end, each received his reward (good or bad), based on how he lived his life.

Life Lessons

I believe the story of Pinocchio will be helpful to illustrate how deceitful the devil is and how easily we fall for his tricks. This tale will also help us understand why it is so important to learn God's voice, much like Samuel did as a young boy, and why we must not seek only selfish pleasures like Eli's sons, Hophni and Phinehas.

Pinocchio was a wooden puppet who came to life as the result of his creator's prayer. Though he was alive, he was still wooden. He wanted very badly to become a real boy; however, he was much more like a real boy than he grasped at the time. Instead of going to school as he was supposed to, he let a sly fox lead him into a puppet show that appeared to be a more exciting adventure. In reality, the adventure was a trick that could have led to a life of hopelessness. After a few minutes of being the star of the show, Pinocchio became trapped, a prisoner of the puppeteer who bought him from the fox. His assigned guardian helped him escape from the puppeteer's "jail." Unfortunately, Pinocchio did not learn his lesson, and the next day he fell into a more dangerous trap.

How silly and naïve must he be to allow the same fox to deceive him a second time? But then think how often we, as humans, have fallen into similar traps set by our nemesis, the devil. This time, the fox took Pinocchio to an amusement park where there was nothing but fun and games. What greater joy and "heaven" could a kid have than to be presented with this wonderful gift?

However, after hours of fun and games, the kids turned into donkeys. What a great life lesson that is—and so true for each of us, too. A life full of nothing but fun and selfish pleasure turns one into a jackass. (I prefer "jackass" as another term for "donkey" because it better describes what we truly become.) Pinocchio's guardian arrived just in time to save him again. I believe my guardian angel has saved me many times[6]—probably more often than I realize.

Pinocchio returned home to find that his creator (and would be "father") was out looking for him (his "son"). In the end, Pinocchio found his father and became a real boy because he forgot about himself and pursued the love for his creator/father. We, too, can become a "real boy" (a child of God) when we let go of our selfish desires and focus entirely on the love of our Creator/Father.

Are you prepared for God's call? Have you repented of your sins? Have you heard the message of Samuel calling you to turn to God? The way we turn to God is through Jesus, our Savior, who died for our sins. If you have never truly accepted Jesus as your Savior, I hope you will invite him into your heart by praying a simple prayer:

Father God, I need and want you in my life, and I am truly sorry for my sins and for all of the things I have done wrong. I believe Jesus died for all of my sins and rose again on the third day. I accept him as your Son and my Savior. Amen.

Yes, a simple prayer such as this, when said with sincerity, will put you right with God and allow you to spend eternity with our heavenly Father and his Son, Jesus. When we are confronted with this world's fun and selfish pleasures, our only hope is through our Savior, Jesus Christ, who died and rose again to save us. Be prepared today.[7]

For Further Discussion

- Discuss how discipline is good for the entire family.
- Have you ever heard the voice of God? Perhaps you did not hear words like Samuel. Maybe you heard him as an inner voice or as a good word from a friend or in a preacher's sermon. Learn to listen for the voice of Jesus. See the scripture references below where Jesus tells us that his people hear his voice and follow him. His voice may not come in ways we would expect; therefore, we need to listen carefully so that we do not miss it when he speaks to us.
- What lesson can you learn from the story of Pinocchio that will help you become disciplined to do the things that are good for you, even when it may not seem like much fun?

For Further Study

1. Hebrews 12:5–10—From Proverbs 3:11, the writer quotes, "My son, do not regard lightly the discipline of the Lord . . . For those whom the Lord loves he disciplines." If you are without discipline, then you are illegitimate children and not sons. Furthermore, we had earthly fathers to discipline us, and we respected them. God (the Lord) disciplines us for our good so that we may share his holiness.
2. John 10:14, 27—Jesus told the people, "I am the good shepherd; I know my sheep and my sheep know me. My sheep listen to my voice; I know them and they follow me."
3. John 10:4–5—Jesus' sheep follow him because they know his voice. They will never follow a stranger; in fact, they will run away if they do not recognize the stranger's voice.
4. John 10:7–10—Jesus said, "I am the gate for the sheep . . . Whoever enters through me will be saved. However, the thief (the devil) comes only to steal, kill, and destroy; I have come that they may have life and have it abundantly."

5. Psalm 103:12–13—As far as the East is from the West, so far has he removed our transgressions from us. Just as a father has compassion on his children, so God has compassion on those who fear him.
6. Matthew 18:10—Jesus tells the people that children's angels continually see the face of God [meaning they are available to help the children].
7. Romans 10:8–9—Faith that is *spoken* from the heart, acknowledging that Jesus is Lord and that God raised Jesus from the dead, will result in salvation (eternal life with God and Jesus).

Chapter 17

SAMUEL TAKES OVER AS LEADER OF THE ISRAELITES

1 Samuel 4–7

As mentioned in the last story, Eli had turned over the priestly duties to his "worthless" sons, Hophni and Phinehas. God spoke to Samuel when he was a young boy, and he reluctantly told Eli of God's plans to punish Eli and his sons; one day soon, they would all die.

In the meantime, the Israelites questioned why they were losing battles with the Philistines. Apparently, they were unaware that God was not pleased with them because they chose to worship other gods in their religious ceremonies. Handicapped by their ignorance, they decided the Ark of the Covenant should go with them into battle. They chose to rely on this symbol of God, rather than relying on God himself. They used the Ark like their enemies used idols, yet God's commandments clearly demanded that they serve *no* idols.

The Ark and the Tabernacle

As you may recall, the Ark of the Covenant was a powerful tool in the right hands. God's power radiated forth from the Ark when it properly resided in the Tabernacle's inner sanctum called the Holy of Holies, which is in the place where the priests of Israel met with God. The Tabernacle was a moveable structure covered by a tent; this was the center of worship for the nation of Israel from the time Moses received God's instructions describing how to build it until the Temple was later built during the reign of King Solomon.

All twelve tribes had participated in building the Tabernacle. Construction began with the foundation. God gave very specific instructions that each family was to contribute exactly the same amount for the foundation; everyone, whether rich or poor, gave one half-shekel.[1] It was only a small amount, so all could afford

139

to give, but it had to be each family's choice. For other parts of the Tabernacle, families gave proportionately according to their wealth.

I believe this is a beautiful picture of our relationship with Jesus. It doesn't matter if we are rich or poor, each and every one of us come to Jesus on equal footing. The only requirement is we must all have the same foundation—that is, our faith in Jesus as our Lord and Savior.[2] The only cost is the same for all; each person must be willing to make the choice to give our heart to Jesus. Any other foundation will fail. The structure built on our foundation and the rewards God gives to each of us are determined by our "spiritual wealth," which comes from those actions and sacrifices in our lives that are given to the glory of God.[3]

Misuse of the Ark of the Covenant

While God's people wanted his blessing, they did not want to serve him according to the Law of Moses; they wanted to serve him in their own way. When the people were disobedient, God withdrew his power, leaving the Israelites vulnerable. Therefore, using the Ark in the way they chose to would be a detriment rather than a help. When the Ark of the Covenant came into the camp of the Israelites, everyone shouted in excitement, for they believed God would now be with them and victory would be theirs. The shouting and celebration was so loud that the noise was heard in the Philistines' camp.

The Philistines became scared; they reminded each other of the previous miracles this Israelite God was responsible for. Sometimes fear paralyzes us, sometimes fear makes us run.[4] And then, sometimes fear can bring out the best in us. The Philistines believed they had no choice but to fight as hard as they could. They feared they would be destroyed, and if they lost, any who survived would be slaves of the Hebrew people. The decision to fight for their lives paid off when the Philistines overwhelmed the Israelites that day in battle.

The Ark was captured by the Philistines, and Hophni and Phinehas were both killed in battle. When the news reached Eli, he was so distraught that he fell over backward, broke his neck, and died. The glory of the Lord was no longer in the Israelites' camp; Samuel's prophesy was fulfilled. Thus, Eli's leadership ended after forty years.

The Philistines were so pleased with their victory that they took the Ark home with them. They wanted their people to know the victory was so great that they captured the Israelites' God. But God would not allow them to celebrate for long.[5] Yes, he was still upset with the Israelites for their evil ways, but he could not let the Philistines believe God could be conquered so easily. The Ark was placed in the house of Dagon, a Philistine god. The next morning, the Dagon statue had fallen on its face. On the second morning, not only had Dagon's statute fallen on its face but also his head and both hands were cut off. The Philistines realized the weakness of their god and never again worshipped Dagon. Of course, they still had other gods to worship.

God was not yet through with the Philistines. Soon, the people of the city where the Ark resided got terrible sores on their bodies. Then mice, often carriers of disease, overtook the city. The Philistines wondered if these horrible sores and afflictions were being caused by the Israelite God. The leaders gathered together

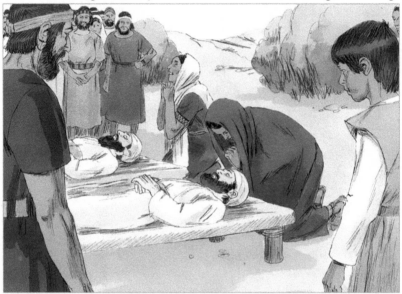

and decided to move the Ark to another city to see if the disease and trouble would affect the new location. It did; and when they moved the Ark to a third city, the epidemic spread throughout the community. Then, the leaders gathered once again and agreed this was the way the Israelites would destroy them. They believed they had no choice but to get rid of this instrument of death; otherwise, the Ark would destroy their entire country.

According to the Philistines, returning the Ark was not a simple task; it had to be done in such a way that the curse would be lifted. The priests of the Philistines devised a plan in which they would build a guilt offering as a way to return the Ark to the people of Israel and remove the curse. They decided to make five golden mice and five golden tumors to represent the sores on their bodies. They made five of each to represent the five major cities of the Philistine people. They hoped this sacrifice would appease the Israelite God. And too, they wanted a final confirmation that the "evil" afflicting their people came from him.

The Philistines hitched the Ark to a cart drawn by two mother cows. They took their calves to their home, which was in the opposite direction of the Israelite city. Then they released the cart with the Ark, the golden tumors, and golden mice to see which direction the cows would go. When the cows headed toward the Israelite city, it confirmed to the Philistines that the Israelite God caused the disease to spread through their nation because the instinct of a mother cow is so strong that she would instinctively take care of her calves first. God was in control of the cart and the cows.

Whose God Is Real?

While all of these practices may seem strange to us in today's world, they provide great insight into the mindset of people from Bible times. Each nation believed they had their own god (or gods) that protected them; therefore, they worshipped their god while believing other nations had their own gods. Oftentimes, nations viewed war not only as a battle between two nations but also a battle between two gods to determine which god was more powerful.

The stories of the Israelite God were well-known all across the land of Canaan. For example, almost everyone knew about the parting of the Red Sea along with the destruction of the powerful Egyptian nation, and they knew of the destruction of the giants in their own land. Apparently, it never dawned on them that they could adopt the Israelite God as their God. None of those who shared the Promised Land with the Israelites understood that there was (is) only one true God. When another god showed its power, they bowed in honor of that god for the moment, but only for a moment. Often, even the Israelites did not understand that they served the *only* true God.

Unfortunately, the Israelites adopted many practices from the surrounding nations. God warned them many times over to separate themselves from these other nations as God's intention was to draw them to himself and teach them that he was the only God. After all, consider the first of the Ten Commandments: "You shall have *no* other gods before me." But the Israelites did not listen. They believed other nations had gods that were powerful and were enticed by some of their immoral practices, often incorporating the pleasurable activities of these other nations into their own worship ceremonies. These actions caused God much anguish and hurt; he had no choice but to disassociate himself from his people and their sinful practices.

Fortunately for the Israelites, God is very merciful. When they eventually repented and turned back to God, he was faithful to forgive and protect them again. But it would be five hundred more years before they understood he was the only true God and finally worshipped him only generation after generation. Even then, they failed to worship him in the proper way. Hence, God designed a way to redeem us (bring us back into his presence) and provided a way to escape the punishment that comes as a result of our sins and failures. He needed at least one man who was able to live a sinless life and offer his life as a perfect sacrifice to pay the price required to cover mankind's sins; and through this perfect sacrifice, this man would stand righteously before God so mankind could be reconciled to him. We know that man did come, and we know him today as God's Son and our Savior, Jesus Christ.[6]

Samuel Becomes Prophet, Priest, and Judge

The nation of Israel was excited to have the Ark back, but they needed to learn that there was much responsibility in caring for the Ark. God is powerful, and he expected the Israelites to worship him in the way he taught them. As a result, many Israelites died before they realized the Ark needed to be in the hands of someone who knew how to present himself before God and properly take care of the Ark in the way God instructed. This finally happened under Samuel's leadership.

Samuel had now reached manhood and was ready to take charge; he became the nation's prophet, priest, and judge:

- **Prophet:** Samuel spoke to all of Israel, saying, "If you return to the Lord with all your heart, remove foreign gods, direct your hearts toward the Lord, and serve him alone, he will deliver you from the hand of the Philistines." So, the Israelites removed the other gods from their worship centers and once again served the Lord alone.

- **Priest:** Samuel prayed for the people, and God's family gathered together at Mizpah, vowing to worship God and acknowledge their sins. God was merciful and forgave them.
- **Judge:** Now, the Philistines heard that the Israelites had gathered in one place and thought they had come together for battle. So, the Philistines prepared to fight. The Israelites cried to Samuel for help. He prayed that God would be with them, and as their judge, Samuel led the Israelites into battle and emerged victorious. Peace reigned again in Israel.

Samuel made peace between God and his people through a special offering to purge the sins that brought calamity from misuse of the Ark and serving other gods. While Samuel made his offering to the Lord, the Philistines approached in battle. With God now reconciled with his people, he intervened, sending a great thunder from heaven that caused great confusion among the Philistine camp and made them run. The Israelites pursued them, and a great victory was won. Samuel built an altar before the Lord to commemorate the victory. The Philistines were subdued that day and did not come within the borders of Israel for all the days of Samuel's leadership. The cities that were previously taken by the Philistines were restored to Israel.

Samuel continued to hear God's voice, and he found favor with God and men. All the days of his life, Samuel delivered messages from God, prayed for Israel, and led them against their enemies as prophet, priest, and judge.

Imagine how different our lives would be if we gathered together as members of God's family to seek forgiveness, both as individuals and as a nation for the sins we have committed.[7] You can start by confessing your sins to God (individually and then with your family) and then commit to seek his will for your life. Take a moment right now to seek what God is calling you to do for him and then act on it. You will feel strength and peace.

For Further Discussion
- Have you ever been so scared you ran from trouble? Has there been a time when you fought harder than ever before because you were scared? Did it work out well?
- You need to be careful not to offend God. He is very patient, but if you cross a line that shows him you are disregarding him, you may find he will demonstrate his power in a way that will make you sorry. Do you think God really does that to people?
- We do not believe in many gods today like the people in Bible times did, but we often "worship" things other than God. What do you worship today that takes your attention away from God?
- Through Samuel's leadership, the people returned to serving God. How does a strong leader help us? What can you do to stay loyal to God? To help others stay loyal?
- In what ways can you seek God and show him that you have chosen to worship him and him alone?

For Further Study
1. Exodus 30:15—The Lord said to Moses, "The rich shall not pay more, and the poor shall not pay less than the half-shekel when you give the contribution to the Lord to make atonement for yourselves." If anyone chose not to give, he could not be numbered as one of the Chosen Family.
2. 1 Corinthians 3:11—For no man can lay a foundation other than the one which is laid in Jesus Christ.

3. 1 Corinthians 3:12–15—Now if any man builds on the foundation with gold, silver, precious stones, wood, hay, and straw, each man's work will become evident; for on that day, fire will test the quality of each man's work. If any man's work, which he has built on it, remains, he will receive a reward. If any man's work is burned up, he will suffer loss; but he himself will be saved through fire (because his foundation is laid in Jesus Christ).

4. Luke 22:54–62—Peter was afraid to let anyone know that he was Jesus' disciple. Then when Jesus saw him after the cock crowed, Peter ran out and wept bitterly.

5. Romans 12:19—Never take your own revenge, but leave room for the wrath of God, for it is written, "Vengeance is mine; I will repay," says the Lord.

6. Hebrews 2:9–10, 17; 10:14—Jesus' death on the cross saved us from death (spiritual death or separation from God). Because Jesus became a man and suffered for us, he was able to be our merciful priest and take our sins away. Through his offering, Jesus perfected believers for all time.

7. Jeremiah 29:11–13—God has plans to give his people a future and a hope. He says, "If you will call upon me (in repentance) and pray to me, I will listen to you. You will seek me and find me when you search for me with all your heart."

Chapter 18

ISRAEL GETS A KING

1 Samuel 8–10

In our last story, we learned how Samuel led the Israelites back into a relationship with God and taught them how to worship God in the way he intended. As Samuel got older, he turned his duties over to his sons. However, they did not walk in the ways of Samuel. They were more interested in dishonest gain; they took bribes and gave justice to those who did not deserve it. As a result, the leaders came to Samuel to complain and to demand a king like the nations around them.

God's Way or the World's Way
God wanted his family to be different than all other nations. He expected

them to look to him as their king. But once again, the Israelites were heavily influenced by their neighbors, which was the very thing God tried so hard to get them to avoid. Because he knew it would be difficult for his family not to fall into the evil ways of Canaan, God cautioned them many times to separate themselves and look *only* to him and fellow family members.

If God's people had been faithful to him, he would have provided constant protection. Why was it so difficult for the Israelites to remain faithful to God alone? Why couldn't they see that the practices of their neighbors were actually harmful and led to destruction? Because evil practices have a pleasurable side that entices us to join in. When we hear the word "evil," it sounds bad. But evil only looks bad after the deed is done. We see pleasure and fun up front; the ugliness only comes out in the end. Remember what happened to Pinocchio when fun and pleasure were the goals? Also, in earlier stories, we learned that the world we live in is under Satan/the devil's rule.[1] So we need to listen to what God tells us is evil and what he tells us is pleasurable and fun. Yes, God wants us to have fun and pleasure; it just needs to be according to his ways. Why do we think we know better than God?

It is easy to be lured into Satan's trap. We are often blinded by the wonderful but temporary thrill from an illegal drug or by the beauty of a woman or by the strong shoulder of a man, especially when our spouse made us angry or did not take the time to understand our issue. Even a video game or fantasy football league can turn into an evil pleasure if we choose to spend all of our free time playing the games. Too often, we prefer the temporary pleasures of this world over the long-term rewards God has in store for all who are willing to be obedient and follow his ways. We cannot imagine the wonders God has in store for those who trust in him. Too often, we want the benefit/reward *now*.

As Samuel entered this later phase in his life, he felt that people were rejecting him, but God explained it was not Samuel they were rejecting; instead, they were rejecting God. The people wanted a king they could see and touch. God forewarned them that a king was not the right answer. A king would command some of their sons and daughters to be his slaves; he would tax them and use the money for his own pleasures; and in some cases, he would even take over their lands for his own personal use. Yes, he would build an army to protect his nation, but he would never be able to protect his subjects as well as God could. Yet, the people would not listen and demanded they have a king like all the other nations. So, God gave the people what they wanted.

We, too, can be hardheaded and insist on doing things our own way. We think we know best, but when things go wrong, we complain and do not under-

stand—some even blame God. God does not make us sacrifice because he wants us to suffer; instead, he asks us to follow his ways because he knows in the long run we will reap the rewards he has in store for us. God does not look at what is best for today or tomorrow or maybe even for this lifetime; God considers what is best for us for eternity.

While it is difficult for our minds to comprehend, this short period of eighty to one hundred years we live on earth is insignificant compared to the eternal life that will come after our earthly existence. For God sees clearly what we cannot see at all. He asks us to trust him and learn to "walk by faith, not by sight;"[2] that is, to "lean not on our own understanding, but acknowledge God in all our ways, and he will make our paths straight."[3] But too often, we insist on doing it our way. As a result, God allows us to live our lives the way we choose, and he will be there to pick us up once we turn to him and follow his paths. Can you think of a time you got something you really wanted and later were sorry that you asked for it?

God Introduces Saul to Samuel

Just because God knew having a king was a mistake did not mean he would not find them a good leader. He searched all over Israel and found Saul, a man from the tribe of Benjamin. Saul was a strong, good-looking man who would command the attention of the people. He was a head taller than any of the other men. Although he was not from a rich family, or even a well-known family, he was fully capable of leading his nation against the enemy. Saul's father, Kish, was also a man of valor, and he passed this trait to his son.

God commissioned Samuel to anoint Saul as king over the nation of Israel, God's own family. Saul was on a journey for his father to find his lost herd of donkeys. After many unsuccessful days of searching, Saul was ready to go home empty-handed, but his servants suggested that they first go to the prophet,

Samuel, who could hear from God to learn where the donkeys were. Without knowing it, Saul's servants were part of God's plan. We, too, can serve as God's instrument to lead others to him in natural and ordinary ways. This will happen when we are following God's will for our lives; like Saul's servants, sometimes we perform God's work without even realizing it.

As Saul entered the city where Samuel resided, God spoke to Samuel, saying, "This is the man whom I have appointed to be king over my people." What a surprise for Saul! He came into the city looking for lost donkeys; he left having been anointed king. God has many blessings for us, often beyond what we can think or imagine—if only we are willing to be obedient and follow him.[4] We think of ourselves as ordinary folks, but in reality, we are very special people. All of God's people will one day be treated like kings. God's Son, Jesus, lived a perfect, sinless life as a man, and he will inherit the entire heavenly realm. Accordingly, he has chosen to share his throne with each of us who become children of God. Whatever Jesus inherits, we inherit.[5] In the meantime, if you truly seek God, you will receive many blessings along the path to inheriting your heavenly throne.

Saul Becomes King

Without Saul telling Samuel why he came to see him, Samuel said, "Your donkeys that were lost have now been found, so do not worry; spend the night here, and tomorrow I will tell you why you are such an honorable person." Saul was stunned when Samuel complimented him. Saul asked, "Why would you speak so highly of someone from a lowly family within the tribe of Benjamin?" Instead of answering him, Samuel took Saul into the banquet that he planned and placed Saul at the head of the table. Saul still had no idea what was in store for him. The next morning, Samuel called Saul before him and gave special instructions. As Saul followed Samuel to the edge of the city, Samuel took a flask of oil and pronounced, "The Lord has anointed you ruler over his people." Saul was king, chosen by God, but it would not be official until he was presented to the people at his formal coronation.

Samuel then shared what would happen to Saul when he returned home so that he would know this pronouncement was truly from God. First, men would tell him the donkeys had been found and then others would give him two loaves of bread and a jug of wine that he was to accept as an offering. Next, he would meet a group of prophets; God's Spirit would fall upon him, and Saul would prophesy with them. This would signify that he had become a new man and God's designated king of Israel.

As Saul turned to leave Samuel, "God changed Saul's heart," meaning God gave Saul the strength and knowledge to be king over his people, and God's

Spirit fell upon him. Once again, God is painting a picture for us through this story of Saul becoming king. In a similar way, we join the family of God. By accepting Jesus' death and resurrection as God's way of reconciling us back to him, we become a new person,[6] molded and set apart for God. And one day, we will be a ruler with Jesus in God's family.[7] God will change our heart, too.

And it happened as Samuel said it would. Two men met Saul, saying that the donkeys had been found and now his father was worrying about what had happened to him. Then three men met Saul and gave him two loaves of bread and a jug of wine. As Saul turned toward home, he came across a group of prophets. The Spirit of God came mightily upon him, and Saul prophesied. The people wondered how it was that Saul came to be speaking God's word among the prophets. As Saul reached home, his uncle questioned him about his journey. Saul shared all that had happened, except he did not mention that Samuel had anointed him to be the king of Israel.

Are you willing to humble yourself like Saul did so that God can change your heart? If so, just as God's Spirit fell upon Saul, so, too, the Holy Spirit will fall upon you, and you will become a child of God. At this point in his life, Saul saw himself as a lowly, humble man, but God saw what he could become. God took this willing servant and gave him a new life with much responsibility. God expected a lot from Saul, but he also promised to be with him—if only Saul would continue to follow God's instructions and plans. God has special plans for you, too. Will you take the time to ask him and be willing to follow what he tells you?

Soon after, Samuel gathered all the tribes of Israel together and gave the people one final chance to reject the idea of having a king. But when the people continued to demand that they needed a king to rule over them, it was time for the official coronation. Samuel went before each tribe until the tribe of Benjamin was selected. Then he went before each family from the tribe of Benjamin until Saul, the son of Kish, was chosen. It was well known that the tribe of Benjamin was one of the weaker tribes in Israel. Years earlier, the entire tribe, except six hundred men, was wiped out because of their wickedness. Thus, it was a surprise that this tribe was selected. But we need to remember, God sees everything from his eternal perspective, which is quite different from our worldly view.

While Samuel was narrowing down his selection, Saul was in hiding; he was still uncomfortable going from a lowly man in a lowly tribe to being a king. But when Samuel presented Saul to the people, they saw a leader, a handsome man who was head and shoulders taller than any of his countrymen. This public

approval gave Saul the confidence he needed; he was now transformed and ready to assume his duties as king. The people cheered, and Saul was crowned king. The people shouted, "Long live the king!"

Are you ready to humble yourself and be a king? Just remember, in God's kingdom, the kings are those who serve and are servants of his people. While this concept is contrary to our world's perspective, being God's servant will be greatly rewarded in his kingdom (God's world).

For Further Discussion
- Are you influenced by your friends? Do you want things because everyone else seems to have them and you think you should too?
- Have you gotten something you really wanted but afterwards were sorry that you got it? Was it something you knew God, your spouse, or your parents did not want you to have?
- Do you realize that God intends his power to work through his people, not by him coming down and making a change or miracle happen without using us? Do you understand he *wants* to use *you*?

- Saul became king over God's people. Do you realize in God's kingdom we will all be joint-heirs with Jesus, meaning we will all be like kings?

For Further Study
1. John 12:31; John 14:30—The ruler of this world is Satan/the devil.
2. 2 Corinthians 5:7—Walk by faith, not by sight; that is, listen to what God and his Word (the Bible) says and not what this world tells you.
3. Proverbs 3:5–6—Listen to God. Do not depend on what you know, and he will guide you all the way through life.
4. Ephesians 3:20—We can do things beyond what we can think or imagine according to the power of God that works *through us.*
5. Romans 8:16–17—As children of God, we are joint-heirs with Jesus.
6. 2 Corinthians 5:17–18—Therefore, if anyone is in Christ, he is a new creature. The old things have passed away; behold, new things have come. Now all these things are from God, who reconciled us to Himself through Christ and gave us the ministry of reconciliation.
7. Romans 8:2, 5–6, 14–17—We need to set our minds on things of God (the Spirit) and not on things of the flesh (this world). This will set us apart, and thereby, we become useful to God. As we walk by the Spirit of God, we become the children of God and joint-heirs with Jesus.

Chapter 19

SAUL LEADS ISRAEL TO VICTORY BUT DISAPPOINTS GOD

1 Samuel 11–15

Previously, the people of Israel pleaded with Samuel to ask God to give them a king. Reluctantly, God gave in to the pleas of his people and chose Saul, a strong and valiant man from the tribe of Benjamin. Initially, Saul did not have confidence in himself, but he soon demonstrated the attributes of a great warrior.

After Saul was crowned king, he was immediately tested. A city in Israel, Jabesh-Gilead, was about to be taken over by the Ammonites, a neighboring kingdom. God's people were so afraid, they wanted to surrender before the battle even began. But the Ammonites wanted the people to do more than just surrender; they wanted to disgrace the people by gouging out the right eye of every person in Jabesh-Gilead. The men of the city requested time to think about the demand to surrender and determine if any of their fellow countrymen would come to their rescue.

Saul Shows His Strength as King

When news of this troubling situation reached Saul, the Spirit of God came mightily upon him, and he was filled with righteous anger.[1] Saul called upon all the people of Israel to join him to save their fellow family members in Jabesh-Gilead. Actually, Saul demanded their help by threatening to make them pay dearly for not being loyal to their nation, Israel. When the people responded by sending their strongest and best warriors to assist Saul in battle against the Ammonites, he sent word to the people of Jabesh–Gilead that help was on the way. The Israelites, under Saul's leadership, easily beat the Ammonites, and the people of Jabesh–Gilead were saved.

This bold act of leadership proved Saul worthy as a leader and solidified him as Israel's king; he was able to consolidate the Israelites into one kingdom, with soldiers from all the tribes of Israel. Beginning with Jacob's twelve sons, the people had remained a loosely tied family. While God still saw his people as a family, they had finally become a nation held together as one unit.

Each tribe had its own personality; some tribes were closer than others. The tribes would be similar to various states within the collective United States of America. Certain regions have more in common than others. For example, Southern states tend to bond together as do states in the Northeast. Also, in larger cities across America, it is common to see a cultural concentration of German, Italian, Greek, and Chinese families living together in the same area of the city. But in a time of crisis (like a war), everyone joins together as one unit with a common goal. The Israelites finally achieved this cohesive status.

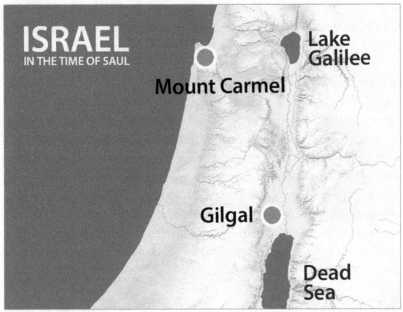

Samuel believed it was time for him to retire and allow Saul to take over as the nation's leader. During Samuel's farewell address, the people confirmed that he had never taken anything from them and had always served them in a worthy and honorable manner. He reminded them how their ancestors repeatedly turned away from God and how they needed to be rescued each time. Now the Israelites wanted a king, so God granted their request—even though he knew they would regret it. God even agreed to look after them, as long as they were willing to follow his laws and serve him and him alone. However, the Israelites would suffer greatly for having a king who would rule over them. They would pay taxes to build the kings' palaces and pay for the other expensive things the kings wanted. The kings would take people from each tribe and make them their servants.

Sometimes we are disobedient, and other times we ask for things God knows are not good for us. When we do, God does not stand in our way. In turn, we must accept that we cannot undo the evil that we bring upon ourselves and our family,[2] and most often, we will suffer the consequences of our poor choices.[3] But just as God did with the Israelites, he promises to be with us and work with us through our poor choices.

Saul was now firmly in control as king of Israel. He established himself by setting up palaces in different cities throughout his kingdom. He was a mighty soldier and leader, and he protected the people in his kingdom. The strongest enemy in Saul's time was the Philistines. After Samuel let his sons take over, this enemy of Israel won most of the battles and took whatever they wanted. But with Saul as king, Israel now had a chance to defend their land.

Saul's First Big Mistake

The Philistines were a strong nation and were surprised by this sudden change of events precipitated by Saul leadership; thus, they began preparations for an all-out war. As the Philistines marched toward Israel, Saul did as God expected: he planned a sacrifice to ask for God's guidance in taking on this powerful enemy. While no longer their judge, Samuel was still the chief priest. He told Saul to wait seven days and he would join him in asking God for guidance. When Samuel did not arrive on the seventh day, Saul saw the fear in his soldiers; some even returned home. Therefore, Saul offered the sacrifice without Samuel, who arrived just as Saul was completing the offering. Samuel asked, "What have you done?" Saul was full of excuses:

> *The people were getting fearful and started heading home; you did not come when you said you would. And besides, the Philistines were assembling; the battle was about to begin. I had no other choice.*

Samuel said, "You have acted foolishly; you have not been obedient to God." As a result, Samuel explained, God would not allow Saul's kingdom to last. God would search for a new king who would seek God with his whole heart. *Wow!* This seems like such a small mistake when God had forgiven his people of much worse. It was not like Saul was not seeking God. Here he was, offering a sacrifice to honor God and ask for his guidance. How could it be so wrong that God would take his kingdom away?

The answer is not always so easy for us to understand. However, as the stories of Saul continue to unfold, we will find out what God already knew; Saul was concerned first and foremost with himself. He had been given riches, power, and strength to protect his family; his only requirement was to listen to and follow God's instructions. Samuel told him to *wait,* and he did—but not long enough. He decided to do it his way.

What a lesson we need to learn! When the enemy is beating down our door and fear begins to come upon us, God may call on us to *wait* until he tells us what to do and how to respond. We are *not* to let overwhelming circumstances take control. But how do we trust someone we cannot see? Do we know for sure he is there? Or if he will ever show up? It is difficult, and it takes a great amount of trust and faith in God to be patient and wait without letting fear take over.[4] God will still forgive you if you do not wait—but as we just learned, we will lose some of our reward—especially if we are given as much as Saul was. To whom much is given, much is required.[5]

God will take care of our enemy or our difficult circumstances. He has his reasons for making us wait. Sometimes he will tell us why, but other times he will leave us in the dark, expecting us to trust him until the time is right. Following God is not always easy, but it is always rewarding to stand firm against the fear that confronts us.

The Philistines attacked, and while they were a mighty army, Saul won the battle. God stood with him as he led his army into battle, but it would never be the same for Saul. As it turned out, he was too concerned about himself and not concerned enough with serving the people God gave him to protect. We will see in this story and in the stories to come that Saul would make one mistake after another—all because he was rash and selfish. This does not mean Saul was all bad; rather, he had a flaw that would eventually take control of him and cause him to lose his kingdom to another man. We will learn this new king would not be perfect either, but he was a man after God's own heart. And that was the centerpiece missing from Saul.

Saul's Son, Jonathan, a True Man of God

An example of Saul's weakness came in the next battle with the Philistines. While everyone was preparing for combat, Saul's son Jonathan decided to seek out his enemy in hopes of finding a place of weakness to attack. Jonathan was one of the valiant warriors by Saul's side in his first great victory. He was also a man of God whose loyalty to his father, to God, and the people he served remained steadfast throughout his lifetime.

Jonathan called for his armor bearer to go with him to spy on his enemy. No one else knew of his plan. As he crossed over a very difficult passageway, he called for God's guidance. Because he wanted to know if God was with him in his quest, he "threw out a trial balloon." As he approached the Philistine guards who were on watch, he told his armor bearer that he would know whether God was with him by what the watchmen said when they saw him climbing up the passageway:

> If the guards say, "Wait until we come to you." Then we will stand in our place and not go up to fight them. But if they say, "Come up to us," then we fight, for the Lord has given them into our hands.

When the Philistines saw Jonathan and his armor bearer, the guards made fun of them because most of the Israelites were hiding in fear of the strong Philistine army. When they told Jonathan to "come up to us," Jonathan proclaimed to his armor bearer, "Come, for God has given them into our hands." The two Israelites fought valiantly and killed twenty men. At this time, God caused the earth to shake. Jonathan's attack, coupled with the earthquake, was such a surprise to the Philistine army that they thought the entire Israelite army had attacked them, so they fled without taking their weapons. Saul's watchmen saw all of this confusion coming from the enemy camp and told Saul, who decided he did not have time to ask God what to do and called for all of his troops to attack the Philistines. Word quickly reached surrounding cities that the Philistines were scared and on the run. So, they, too, joined in the fight.

Since the Philistines ran off without their weapons, Saul wanted every man pursuing the soldiers before they escaped. If he did not get them now, the Philistines might have a chance to regroup, and Israel would lose their chance for total victory. Saul told everyone, "Cursed be the man who eats anything before we avenge our enemies." All were afraid of what Saul would do to the person who disobeyed. But Jonathan was not there to hear the command, so as he continued to fight, he came across a beehive filled with honey and ate some of it. As soon as he ate, his strength returned and his eyes brightened. When Jonathan was told of Saul's order, he said, "How foolish a command. Notice how much strength I gained when I ate; imagine how much greater the victory could have been if the soldiers had been allowed to eat."

That evening after the battle, the people were so famished that they ate the sheep and cows without preparing them properly as the Law of Moses commanded. To counteract their sin, Saul prepared a sacrifice and asked God to forgive the soldiers; he, then, instructed them to properly prepare the food for eating. The next day, Saul asked God if he should continue the fight against the Philistines, but God did not answer him. When it became clear that God was not answering because of a sin committed among the soldiers, Saul went to the people to find out who sinned. The lot fell upon Jonathan because he ate the honey in disobedience to the king's command.

Although it may have been a foolish commandment, a king's decree became law, and a person who broke the law must be punished. If the king made an exception for his own family, it would be considered a weakness, and his kingdom would be vulnerable and could be lost. Therefore, even though the curse was foolish, Jonathan felt compelled to honor it. But the Israelites came to Jonathan's rescue and said this great victory was because of Jonathan and there was no way they would allow him to die. Consequently, Jonathan was spared punishment.

However, Saul lost credibility with God; he was impatient and irrational. First, he should have waited on Samuel; then, his rash command caused his son to sin unknowingly; and finally, he caused the people to sin because they were so starved they failed to follow the laws in properly preparing the food.

Are you going to be like Saul: chosen by God but impatient in waiting on him, making rash decisions and selfishly thinking of only what you want?[6] Or are you going to be like Jonathan: seeking God for victory, willing to follow God's lead, fighting valiantly when given the go ahead, and being loyal enough to accept unmerited punishment for the good of the group?[7] We will see in future stories how Jonathan continued to serve God in many admirable ways. Jonathan's rewards and blessing will be heard and received throughout eternity. Try it his way and see God's blessings come shining forth.

For Further Discussion

- Saul was making a sacrifice to honor God and to ask how he should properly prepare for the upcoming battle. Why do you think God was so upset with him?
- Discuss opportunities/situations where you should take the required punishment, even when you did nothing wrong.
- Discuss the admirable characteristics of Jonathan. How can you learn to be more like him?
- What does the word "humble" mean to you in terms of how you need to live your life?

For Further Study

1. Ephesians 4:26–27—Be angry but do not sin; do not give the devil an opportunity.
2. At times, our sins cause consequences, not only for us but also for generations afterwards. When we participate in communion (the Lord's Supper), Paul says we are to examine our actions and ask for forgiveness; not doing so can cause problems, sickness, and even death:
   a. Exodus 20:5
   b. I Corinthians 11:26–32

3. 1 Peter 2:20; 4:15—There is no need to complain if you are suffering for things you've done wrong.

4. Psalms 37:34—Wait for God. Keep his way, and he will exalt you to inherit the land; you will look on when God takes care of your enemy.

5. Luke 12:47–48—Jesus shares that God does not expect as much from those who do not know better as he does from those who know what to do but do not do it. He says, "From everyone who has been given much, much will be required; and to whom they entrusted much, of him they will ask all the more."

6. James 3:16—For wherever there is jealousy and selfish ambition, there you will find disorder and evil of every kind.

7. Matthew 20:28—For even the Son of Man came not to be served but to serve others and to give his life as a ransom for many.

Chapter 20

DAVID RECEIVES GOD'S ANOINTING

1 Samuel 16

I f God's people were ever going to serve him, they needed a leader and a king who would stand up for God. While Saul exhibited many good qualities, his selfish ways and unwillingness to properly serve God would eventually lead to his family's removal from the monarchy. When Samuel lamented Saul's fall from "grace," God told Samuel to stop grieving and follow him to meet the person he (God) had selected to be king.

God Looks at the Heart, Not the Outward Appearance

God instructed Samuel to go to Bethlehem, a small village in Judah, to visit the family of Jesse. To avoid any suspicion from Saul, Samuel let it be known

that he was going to offer a sacrifice. Samuel invited Jesse and his sons to the sacrifice so that God could show him who would be the next king. As he prepared the offering, Samuel felt certain that Jesse's oldest son, Eliab, would be the one selected to be the next king. He was tall, handsome, and just the sort of person the people would look up to. But God told Samuel not to consider the outward appearance; rather, he should examine a man's heart to determine whether he would be committed to honor and love God.

As each of Jesse's seven sons passed by Samuel, God rejected them. Samuel asked if Jesse had any other sons. When he learned the youngest son, David, was out in the fields tending sheep, Samuel asked Jesse to send for him immediately. As soon as David appeared, God told Samuel, "Arise, anoint him, for he is my king." David, while small in stature, was a handsome young man with beautiful

eyes, yet it was David's heart for God that impressed him (God). As soon as Samuel anointed David with oil, the Spirit of the Lord came upon David and stayed with him from that day forward. Prophetically, this foreshadowed Jesus' receiving the Holy Spirit when he was anointed at his baptism by John.

Can God say the same thing about your heart? Would God be able to look at you from the inside and know that you love him and are ready to serve him? Also, when you choose someone to follow, do you look at the person's outward appearance? Or do you take the time to find out how the person thinks and believes?

Growing up, we likely chose the most popular and best-looking people to be our leaders. I do not believe we always make the best choices in our youth, but sadly, as we get older, our choices rarely improve. We tend to choose leaders who tell us what we want to hear. Frequently, these leaders are more interested in getting re-elected than in making the best choices for those they represent. Consider carefully those with whom you choose to associate; it will make a difference in your life.

King for Eternity

God chose David and his descendants to be king over his people for eternity. For this special family line, God needed a man after his own heart, and David had that special ingredient. But how is David's family king for eternity? We can see this was God's plan when Jacob prophesized (foretold) that the king would come through his son Judah (Volume 1, part 4 of Joseph's story), the direct ancestor of David. We can also see how David was part of God's plan in the stories of Ruth, his great grandmother. We now see the next phase of God's plan unfolding when David became the earthly king. *Not* coincidentally, David is the ancestor of the Virgin Mary, the mother of Jesus, which gives him (Jesus) the earthly right to be king of God's people.[1]

But why did the Son of God need to come to earth as a human? Why couldn't he be king from heaven? Beginning with the sin of Adam and Eve, mankind was separated from God, and the cost of our sin was death. Reconciliation was necessary, but it required mankind's victory over death to overcome our sins. We continually failed by falling short of following God's commandments. However, God wanted to bridge the separation and provide redemption for mankind, so he devised a plan to offer his son as a perfect sacrifice so that we could have eternal life as a free gift through Christ Jesus, our Lord.[2] To accomplish this, Jesus gave up his equality with God to become God's only begotten son (human), and he humbled himself by becoming obedient to the point of death on a cross.[3]

Because of his sinless life, Jesus' perfect sacrifice broke the power of death that the devil held over mankind. With this sacrifice, Jesus paid the price of sin and graciously offered eternal life when he chose to redeem all who believed in him.[4] Therefore, by accepting Jesus as our Savior, we become members of the family of God, with Jesus at the head of the family as king forever.[5] Thus, David's family is king for all eternity.

What a prize for David and his family! And for us, too. When we become part of God's family, we become joint-heirs with Christ,[6] which makes us part of God's royal family. Our goal, then, should be to be like David, whom God proclaimed as a man after God's own heart.[7]

Prophet, Priest, and King

God was now ready to implement a new system of religion and government for Israel in which prophets, priests, and a king would lead the people. (Note: this is the next generation to the system previously shared in chapter 17, Samuel's story.) If everyone played his proper role, peace and harmony would reign in Israel.

- **Prophet:** God spoke to the prophets, who then had the responsibility to deliver the messages and truths God wanted the people to know. Sometimes, the messages were about the future, and often, God called for a corrective action on the part of his people.
- **Priest:** If the people had a request of God, they spoke to the priests, who then offered the prayer to God on the person's behalf; this prayer was accompanied by a sacrifice on an altar. As I shared in Saul's story, he made a major mistake when he got impatient and offered the sacrifice himself, instead of waiting on Samuel, who was the high priest at the time. The priests also offered many sacrifices on a continual basis, asking forgiveness for the many sins of the people.
- **King:** The king ruled over the people; he was the military head and set up the court system to judge the people and their disputes. So, the king was the protector and judge of God's family.

This structure is a picture of the system we will live under in the new heaven and new earth. Jesus will fulfill all three roles as our prophet, priest, and king. Jesus is the head, the leader, and the ruler,[8] but he is also our priest, providing direct access to God any time we need him.[9] The Holy Spirit is given to us to receive God's messages that Jesus, our prophet, shares with us.[10] Jesus told the disciples that he was going away so that he could send us a Comforter (the Holy Spirit), who would not be *beside* us but *inside* us to guide us into all truths.[11]

The Bible describes the Holy Spirit, our Comforter, as equal with Jesus. So, we now have access to God our Father through Jesus, his Son, by the Holy Spirit; thus, we have the Trinity, God three in One. Each are separate beings of the same person, with different roles that come together as one in a way that our human mind cannot easily comprehend. God did not speak through the Holy Spirit to each Israelite the way he does for us now (that would come later after Jesus performed his appointed task: his death and resurrection).

David Lives in the Royal Household

Now back to the story. God was not ready to announce David as king; first, God needed to prepare him for a lifetime of leadership. As the next several stories unfold, we will see how much David went through before God was ready to let it be known that David was his king for Israel.

As the Spirit of the Lord fell upon David, God's Spirit left Saul, and an evil spirit terrorized him. His servants suggested that music would soothe the king's

soul, so they searched the kingdom for a person skilled in playing the harp. It was learned that David, Jesse's son, was a perfect choice. Saul soon loved David so much that not only did he have him play for him, but David also became his armor bearer. This role is usually reserved for a younger person who is given the privilege to go into battle with and carry armor for a person of high rank (in this case, the king). However, David still had responsibilities back in his hometown of Bethlehem to be the shepherd for his family's sheep.

David was now involved in the activities of the royal family. He had a front-row seat from which he could carefully observe the king's responsibilities since they would one day be his. David would soon be placed in the forefront, to help achieve the peace and harmony Israel was striving for. In our next story, we will find out just how involved he would be. In the meantime, I challenge you to surround yourself with people who have a heart for God. Observe what is going on around you so that you may learn what God has in store for you.

For Further Discussion
- God sees us all based on what is going on inside of us (our heart). That is, God views our spiritual health instead of our outward appearance. How do you stack up?
- Are you ready to let Jesus be your:
  - King (humbling yourself before him as your ruler)?
  - Priest (praying to him, knowing he is the only one who can give you access to God)?
  - Prophet (taking time to mediate on and listen to any messages he wants to give you)?
- How can the Holy Spirit be your guide?

For Further Study
1. Luke 3:23–31—The genealogy of Mary, the mother of Jesus, a descendant of King David, is given.
2. Romans 6:23—The wages of sin are death; the free gift of God is eternal life in Christ Jesus.

3. Philippians 2:5–11—Jesus gave up his position in heaven and became a man so he could save us. He died so we could live, and God exalted him above every other name. Now everyone will confess that Jesus is Lord.
4. Hebrew 2:14, 17—Jesus became a man to defeat death and take it away from the devil. To do that, he had to die in place of his brethren (fellow human beings) so that he could be a substitute for the sins of the people.
5. Revelation 11:15—In the end times, the kingdom of the world becomes the kingdom of our Lord, and he will reign forever.
6. Romans 8:16–17—We become the children of God and, thus, joint-heirs to reign with Jesus.
7. Acts 13:22—After God made David king, God testified concerning him: "I have found David, son of Jesse, a man after my own heart; he will do everything I want him to do."
8. Revelation 19:16; 22:3—Jesus' robe will have the name "King of Kings" written on it. God's throne will be in the new heaven, and the Lamb (Jesus) will sit on the throne.
9. Hebrews 7:17, 22–27—For it is declared, "You are a priest forever, in the order of Melchizedek." In the old covenant, multiple priests were needed as the death of each required a replacement, but Jesus continues forever as he holds his priesthood permanently.
10. Acts 3:22–24—Moses foretold of the coming Prophet (Jesus), to whom all will give heed or be destroyed.
11. John 16:7, 13—Jesus told his disciples it was to their advantage that he leave them as he would send a Helper, and when the Helper (the Holy Spirit) came, he would guide them (and us) into all truth.

⌒

Chapter 21

DAVID CONFRONTS GOLIATH

1 Samuel 17

⌒

Our next story begins after Samuel, under God's direction, anointed David to be the king of Israel. But the anointing was done in secret because David would not officially become the king until Saul died or was removed. In the meantime, David was appointed as harpist to play for the king when the evil spirits attacked Saul's mind and sent him into a rage. Not only did David's playing settle the king's spirit, but David's personality captured the hearts of the king and his family—particularly the heart of Jonathan, the king's oldest son.

A Philistine Giant Challenges Israel's Manhood

Not so long after David began playing the harp for Saul, the Israelites were in a major battle with the Philistines. One of the Philistine leaders, a giant named Goliath, challenged the Israelites to a one-on-one battle with him. He said it was foolish to kill so many of each army. He asked, "Why not let one person from each army fight it out, with the losers becoming slaves for the victorious side?" This does not sound like a fair fight since Goliath was not only a giant but also a great warrior.

Goliath was an impressive sight. He was almost ten feet tall and wore a bronze helmet with a suit of armor that weighed 125 pounds. He had a bronze javelin slung across his chest, carried a spear with a head that weighed fifteen pounds, and had a large sword tucked in his belt. Who would be stupid enough to accept his challenge?

All of Israel's soldiers cringed each morning as Goliath came to the center of the battlefield to challenge and degrade the Israelites. And each day, Goliath came forth more confidently than before, knowing the Israelites were becoming

more and more afraid of him. He believed no one would accept his challenge, but it would serve to belittle the Israelites so much that when it came time for the actual battle, they would crumble before Goliath and his fellow Philistine soldiers. Saul offered great riches and Merab, his daughter, in marriage to any man who took on Goliath and was victorious. Of course, no one was willing to risk his life for a battle he was sure to lose. Or was there someone? Let's find out.

At times, we are faced with problems that seem far bigger and more difficult than we can handle. It is on just such an occasion that we must learn to rely on God. We have to let him take over.[1]

While Goliath was challenging the Israelites to one-on-one combat, David was back home tending his father's sheep, but three of his oldest brothers were in Saul's army. When Jesse became concerned about his sons, he sent David to the battlefront with food for his brothers and his brothers' commanders. Jesse was smart to include a gift for his sons' commanders. This little "bribe," given in the right way, could help the commanders treat Jesse's sons favorably, and thus, according to the Book of Proverbs, be a benefit both to the giver and the receiver.[2]

You might think of how you can use this practice to your advantage in all walks of life, whether offering a simple compliment to tell a lady how nice she looks, a little gift to say thank you, or an act of kindness. You never know when someone may repay your kindness with something you need.

David Stands Up for God

When David arrived at the battlefield, he observed what was going on and wondered why the Israelites were letting Goliath speak against them without accepting his challenge. David said, "Who is this uncircumcised Philistine that he should taunt the armies of the living God? If none of you are willing to take on this giant, I will." David's oldest brother was very angry with him and said, "With whom have you left the sheep? I know your insolence and the wickedness of your heart; you just wanted to see the battle." In essence, David's brother was saying, "You little brat, who are you to come here to criticize your elders and put us down in this way? You have no idea what you are talking about." David naively said, "What have I done now? Was it not just a question?"

Doesn't this sound just like two brothers fussing with one another? David's brother may have felt that David was making them look bad, or maybe he was jealous; sometimes older brothers just like to put down a younger one. But, on some level, his brother had a point. David had never experienced the fear and anxiety that come with facing death and seeing your fellow soldiers die horribly right before your eyes. How do you think you might react as the younger brother? What if you were the older brother?

However, in this case, David was speaking the truth. When the other soldiers saw how sincere David was, they took him to Saul. But Saul was concerned, "You are not able to go against this Philistine; you are but a youth, and he is a warrior well-seasoned." David responded to Saul by sharing how he had confronted danger before:

> *When a lion attacked my sheep, I rescued the sheep from his mouth; and when the lion turned against me, I seized him by his beard and killed him. And I will do the same to the Philistine who has taunted the armies of the living God. God, who delivered me from the jaws of the bear and lion, will deliver me from the hand of the Philistine.*

What a bold and confident young man who, we discover, was one with God! Remember, when he was anointed by Samuel, the Holy Spirit came upon him. David knew he would be victorious because God was with him. How can you learn or become confident that God will be with you in difficult circumstances? It is important to always remember that, as a believer, you, too, have the Holy Spirit inside you, fighting with you and for you.[3]

Saul tried to help David by giving him his own armor, but Saul's armor was too big for David, who was much smaller than Saul. However, David was not dismayed. He chose his weapon, a sling shot with five smooth stones he picked up from a brook running through the valley.

Years ago, my wife, Nan, and I went to Israel. One of the places we visited was the valley where David fought Goliath. I went into the same brook that

David crossed and picked out five smooth stones. We brought them home with us. A few months later, Nan took the stones to church to show her choir of five-year-olds and to share with them the story of David and Goliath.

When she got to the part where David picked up the stones from the brook, she reached in her bag and pulled out our five smooth stones and said that we got them from the very same brook where David got his stones. One of the children stood up in the middle of her story and exclaimed, "Wait a minute! Are you telling me these stories are about real people?" It has always amazed me how these five stones made the story real to this young child. David was real. So is Jesus. It is not just a story. We need to be like this young child and truly grasp that God is real and ready and willing to be an intimate part of our lives.

As David approached Goliath, the Philistine looked with disdain on the youth. In disgust, Goliath said, "Am I a dog that you come to me with sticks?" He cursed David by the name of his false gods and said he would give David's flesh to the birds and beasts. David showed he was still confident:

You come to me with sword, spear, and javelin, but I come to you in the name of God, whom you have taunted. This day, God will deliver you into my hands, and I will strike you down, remove your head, and deliver it to the birds and the beasts.

While it is true that this is rough language, David was upset to hear Goliath mocking God. He was determined to show Goliath that God was the one in control.

David was not capable in his own strength, but he knew he could do all things through God, who would strengthen him.[4] Proudly, David told Goliath that God was making a statement by allowing such a small man with a small weapon to conquer the great man of the Philistines. David said, "Everyone will know that the battle was the Lord's and that he gave you into our hands."

David Battles Goliath

As Goliath came to the middle of the battlefield, David quickly ran to meet him. David reached into his bag and took one of the stones and slung it, striking Goliath between his eyes. The stone sank into the giant's forehead, and he fell on his face. David took Goliath's sword, and as promised, David cut off Goliath's head and held it high for all to see. When the Philistines saw their champion was dead, they fled. The men of Israel arose and chased after the Philistines, winning a great victory. With Goliath's head in hand, David arrived in Jerusalem, proudly showing the conquered warrior for all to see. David was brought to Saul to be honored before Israel.

Why did David select five stones? It only took one to kill Goliath. A friend of mine believes David needed four additional stones because Goliath had four brothers. If this were true, he would need to be prepared for the other brothers in case they attacked after he killed Goliath. Much later, the Bible describes where four Philistine giants were killed by men in David's army, which helps to support my friend's belief.[5]

God expects us to do our job and prepare for every circumstance when we go into battle—including things in everyday life. This is true whether we are preparing for an important meeting at work, a final exam at school, or a championship football game. God promises to be there with us and for us, but you will not pass the test if you do not study or properly prepare for the big event. Sometimes preparation means you have to give up something you want to do to be ready for the job.

We, too, can be confident that we can win the battle and overcome the problems we face in this life. But we need to turn to God in the way David did by allowing God's Spirit to come upon us. How do we do this? By giving Jesus control of our life. When I shared this with my granddaughter, who was eleven at the time, she said, "Papa, that's scary!"

Boy, did she get it! It is scary to let someone else take control—even more so when we cannot physically see God. You can no longer do it your way; you must do it God's way. When you **give your life to God and recognizing his sovereignty**, you have learned the **first lesson** in becoming disciplined and under God's control. And you will never be sorry; the blessings you receive will far outweigh any sacrifices you make for God.

Jesus has an answer for those times we are overwhelmed with life and the problems we face. He said, "Come to me all who are weary and heavy laden, and

I will give you rest. Take my yoke upon you and learn from me, for my yoke is easy and my burden is light."[6] Jesus will be there for us, but we have to put on his "yoke;" that is, we have to give him control. I pray that at some point we, like David, will one day declare to the enemy (or problems) we face, "How dare you taunt the living God?" And you, too, will be ready to cut off the head of the evil that confronts you.

As I expressed above, you have now learned the first of ten lessons in becoming disciplined and under God's control. As I continue to share these exciting but often challenging adventures of David, we will learn additional lessons in how to let God take control of our lives.

For Further Discussion

- Paraphrasing, David, in essence, told Goliath, how dare you taunt the people of God? I have come to defend his name, and God will deliver me—no matter how big you are. Have you ever had the opportunity to stand up for God when others were discounting who God is and the power he has?
- What kind of giant (major problem) have you faced in your life? Did you let God take control?
- Have you thought about what it means to give Jesus control of your life? By taking on Jesus' yoke (Matthew 11:29), you are giving him the reins to control your life. It may be scary, but it will be the best decision you ever make. Are you willing?

For Further Study

1. Psalms 37:5, 9–10—Commit your way to the Lord; trust in him. For those who are evil will be destroyed, but those who hope in the Lord will inherit the land. After a little while, the wicked will be no more; though you look for them, they will not be found.
2. Proverbs 17:8—A bribe is a charm in the hand of its owner; wherever he turns, he prospers.
3. Romans 8:11; John 16:13—The Spirit who raised Jesus from the dead dwells in you. He (the Spirit) will guide you into all the truth.

4. Philippians 4:13—I can do all things through him (Jesus) who gives me strength.

5. 2 Samuel 21:15–22—This story tells how, under his leadership, David's men killed four giants; at least one was the brother of Goliath (verse 19). Since verse 22 says these four were born to the giant in Gath, it would be consistent to say all four were brothers of Goliath.

6. Matthew 11:28–30—Jesus encourages us to come to him with all of our problems and concerns. He will give us rest, but we are called to put on his yoke so that he can guide us. To put on his yoke means to be under his control.

Chapter 22

DAVID AND JONATHAN

1 Samuel 18–20

After his victory over Goliath, David became known throughout Israel, much the same as people become famous today. Saul honored David and regularly brought him to eat at his table, which was a special honor given to few people outside the royal family. David became a leader in Saul's army and was responsible for many victories. With each victory, David became more "famous" and pleasing in the sight of the people of Israel. His victories were especially rewarding to the Israelites after years of being servants to the Philistines.

The women of Israel celebrated by dancing and singing songs about the victories of King Saul and David: "Saul has slain his thousands and David his ten thousands." The chorus rang in Saul's ears; however, instead of feeling proud of all the victories and realizing that David was truly his humble servant, Saul became jealous and distrustful of David. He saw the love his people poured out toward David and was concerned that the people wanted David to be king. Saul was also afraid that David may want to take over his kingdom. As we learned in earlier stories, kings relied heavily on their advisors, and while the Bible does not specify in this instance, it is quite likely that Saul's advisors were cautioning him that David may decide he should be king. Such takeovers were a common occurrence in Bible times.

If Saul had been willing to hear from God, he would have accepted David's loyalty to his king. Saul needed only to recognize and accept God's gift. Instead, he let his fears control his emotions and actions. As a result, his heart became troubled, and God's peace left him. Jesus has called us to a different life.[1] Are you ready to let go of your own desires and let God rule in your heart? If so, you must learn to heed God's advice.

Friendship and Honor

Saul's son Jonathan grew to admire David, and they became very close friends. The Bible says the soul of Jonathan was knit to the soul of David, and Jonathan loved David as himself. David felt the same toward Jonathan, and together they made a covenant to support and honor each other and to take care of each other's family. As the first-born son of Saul, Jonathan was in line to be king after Saul. While we do not know how or when, the Bible makes it clear that Jonathan understood that God's plan was for David, instead of him, to be the next king of Israel.

You may recall from one of our earlier stories that Jonathan himself was a valiant warrior. He had proven himself on the battlefield and looked to God for guidance and support. He was everything you would want in a soldier. And beyond that, he had all the attributes of an impressive leader and a mighty king, yet he did not let this stand in his way of his relationship with David or cloud his knowledge that David would one day be king in his place. Jonathan had every right to be king. And by all earthly standards, he should have guarded himself against David and done everything to protect his right to the throne. But instead, he humbled himself and became David's servant. This is the **second lesson** in becoming disciplined and under God's control: **put the needs of others in front of your own**.[2]

Jonathan was also a faithful servant to his father, Saul. As Saul became more and more jealous of David, Jonathan had the difficult task of balancing his friendship with David and his loyalty to his father. Yet he always seemed to balance the two positions in a respectful and honorable way.

Jonathan's attitude and actions are great examples for us to follow; he displays characteristics we see in Jesus. Just as Jonathan was willing to give up his right to be king, choosing instead to be David's humble servant, the New Testament Book of Philippians tells us Jesus gave up his godly powers (but not his divine nature) to become a man. In obedience to his Father's request, Jesus humbled himself to suffer and die on the cross in order that mankind could be saved. As a result, God exalted him and proclaimed, "In that day, every knee will bow and every tongue confess that Jesus Christ is Lord."[3]

Moreover, Jonathan demonstrates how we should live as we face life's issues and problems. Let's see how the story unfolds.

David Becomes Part of the Royal Family

To set up the next sequence of events, let's review David's history with Saul. Saul had disappointed God so often that God had Samuel secretly anoint David as God's king. The Spirit of the Lord left Saul, and an evil spirit took over, causing Saul much stress and anxiety. Since his teenage years, David soothed the soul of Saul with music, playing his harp when Saul's fears and anxiety became overwhelming. As a result, Saul and his entire household came to know David very well. Everyone liked him, even as a young teenager before his battle with Goliath.

Imagine the torment all of this caused Saul. He had grown to love David; he was proud of David's victory over Goliath and all the victories over the Philistines that made his kingdom secure. And yet, at the same time, Saul knew that God had abandoned him. He recognized that David may take over his kingdom, and he was afraid it would happen at any moment.

One day while David was playing his harp, an evil spirit came mightily upon Saul. He threw a spear at David, thinking he could "pin David to the wall" and thereby eliminate his competition for the kingdom. However, David was able to move quickly enough that Saul's spear just missed him.

In other attempts to get rid of his competition, Saul sent David into the fiercest combat zones, hoping he would lose his life on the battlefield. However, this tactic backfired on Saul. Under David's leadership, all the tribes of Israel continued to prosper, especially Judah (David's home tribe), and the people loved David all the more.

So, Saul tried another ploy. When Saul learned of his daughter Michal's love for David, he decided to use her affection to his advantage and offered her in marriage to David on one condition. Before sharing that condition, it is interesting to note that Saul had already promised that whoever killed Goliath would win not only a rich financial reward but also his daughter Merab as a wife. This marriage would have made David his son-in-law and, thus, a member of the royal family. However, Saul conveniently chose not to honor that part of his agreement after David killed Goliath and instead gave Merab in marriage to another man.

Since David was a commoner without sufficient funds to pay the price of a princess, Saul asked David to personally kill one hundred Philistines as his dowry (price) for Michal. David took on the task as an honor and brought back evidence that he killed *two* hundred Philistines, thus causing Saul even more grief as he had to honor his offer and give Michal to David as his wife. So, once again, Saul's plan backfired, and David was now officially part of the royal family, giving Saul even more reason to fear him.

Michal was pleased to become David's wife. Isn't it wonderful how God allows something to happen that appears to go against us and then we later learn that it works in our favor? By not demanding that Saul give Merab as promised, David eventually married the daughter who truly loved him.[4]

Jonathan Demonstrates His Friendship

While God allowed Saul's reign as king to continue, he wasn't going to let it be easy. Even the Philistines held high regard for David because of his wisdom and valor in battle.

Where does Jonathan fit into all of this? As I previously mentioned, he was torn between his friendship with David and his loyalty to his father. Jonathan remembered how much his father loved David early on, so it was difficult for him to believe Saul could do anything but have respect for all that David had done to help secure his kingdom. Then one day, Saul told Jonathan and his servants to put David to death. Jonathan encouraged David to find a hiding place and told him he would try to get his father to change his mind. Once things settled down, Jonathan promised to let David know that it was safe to return.

Jonathan reminded Saul of all the wonderful things David had done—how he killed Goliath and won many battles against the Philistines—and reminded him how much love David had for all of Saul's family and how David had nothing but respect and loyalty for Saul and his reign. Saul listened and vowed to change his attitude. Jonathan saved the day.

Therefore, David temporarily returned to the palace, playing the harp to soothe Saul's tormented soul. However, it was not long before the evil spirit took over, and Saul once again threw his spear, just missing David. He fled, and the next day Saul was after David with a vengeance. With Michal's help, David escaped through a window in the palace wall. She placed a household statue in his bed to make it look like David was asleep, giving him enough time to escape. David went to Samuel for protection since he was still a man of great respect among the nation of Israel and was feared by Saul.

Saul learned of David's hiding place and sent messengers to bring him back to the palace. But the messengers were overcome by the Spirit of God; they started prophesying (speaking words from God), and their mission to retrieve David was aborted. When Saul learned of this, he sent additional messengers, but the same thing happened. Finally, Saul went to capture David himself, but the Spirit of the Lord came upon him, and Saul, too, began prophesying. We are not told what the messengers or Saul spoke when they declared the words of God, but the message to us is that we cannot go against God's will when we are speaking God's words. And it was not God's will to bring harm to his chosen king, David. As a result, Saul repented before the Lord, and in the morning, he returned home without David.

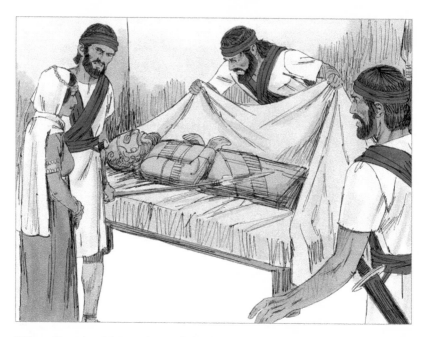

When David told Jonathan of the latest events, Jonathan could not believe it, for by now, Saul had again repented and was no longer after David. But David knew it was God who caused Saul to prophesy and return without capturing him. In other words, David knew the reprieve was only temporary. Jonathan was skeptical but optimistic that his father truly loved David and would want him back in his household. So, Jonathan and David devised a plan to find out for sure how Saul felt.

Jonathan suggested that David stay hidden during the first day of the Jewish festival that was to be celebrated the next day. All the family members would be expected to attend the meal, so if David was not there, Saul would surely comment. Jonathan planned to tell Saul that David's oldest brother required him to be with his family in Bethlehem. If Saul accepted this explanation, then Jonathan would know Saul's attitude and feelings toward David were healthy. But if Saul got angry, he would know that his father still intended to have David killed.

Jonathan promised that he would not take his father's side in this matter because he knew the love David had for his family, including Saul. Jonathan and David made a final covenant with each other that no matter what happened, they would forever support each other, and if something happened to one of them, the survivor would take care of the other person's family.

David told Jonathan where he would be hiding, and on the third day of the festival, Jonathan would leave to practice his bow and arrow. If Saul was speaking favorably of David, Jonathan would tell his servant, "The arrows are closer, so come toward me," but if Saul was still angry, he would tell his servant, "The arrows are beyond you." In this way, David would know that he must leave the city and find a more permanent hiding place.

David Must Escape

On the first day of the festival, Saul did not say anything, thinking David stayed away to purify himself before the Lord. When David did not show up the second day, Saul inquired of Jonathan regarding David's absence. Jonathan explained that David had requested to be with his family in Bethlehem. When Saul heard Jonathan's response, he burned with anger and said to his son, "You have chosen to be on the side of my enemy, David; you should be ashamed of yourself." He explained that Jonathan would never be king as long as David was alive and demanded that Jonathan bring David to him. But Jonathan argued, saying, "What has David done to you?" In his anger, Saul picked up his spear and threw it at Jonathan. Jonathan now knew there was no hope for any reconciliation between David and Saul. Jonathan spent the rest of the day fasting and grieving over his father's attitude and the loss he would experience now that David had to leave.

The next day, Jonathan went to the appointed place with his servant and shot three arrows in the field. As the servant reached the place of the arrows, Jonathan said, "Aren't the arrows beyond you?" After the servant brought the arrows to Jonathan, he sent him home. David came out of hiding, and both he and Jonathan wept together. He told David, "Go in safety and remember that we have sworn to each other in the name of the Lord that we will support each other forever."

As much as Jonathan hated to lose David, he knew his place and responsibility was by his father's side. This did not mean that he agreed with his father; in fact, he was very upset with him, but as the king in waiting, he had certain

responsibilities to fulfill. He honored his father as far as he could but not to the point he was willing to deliver an innocent man to his father to be killed.

Jonathan is truly an example of how we are supposed to live our life for God. He knew that by allowing David to live, he would not be king, but he also knew God's plans and was willing to submit to them. He was willing to put David's own good ahead of his wishes or ambition.[5] At the same time, he also followed the Ten Commandments, which say we are to honor our father and mother. We will see in a later story that Jonathan stands with his father, even to the end, as they died together in battle against the Philistines.

This story has centered around Jonathan's commitment both to David and his father, Saul. In later stories, we will learn about David's turn to honor God by waiting on God's timing to become king. David would in no way fight against Saul, no matter how badly Saul treated him. And too, we will see how David takes care of Jonathan's family just as he promised. These two young men are great examples of what it means to be part of the family of God. At this point, it was necessary for Jonathan to put David's needs ahead of his own. We cannot do this without letting God be in control because our natural instinct would be to take care of ourselves first.

Are you willing to follow the example of these two "brothers in Christ"? Are you ready to embrace this second lesson in becoming disciplined and under God's control: putting the needs of others ahead of your own needs?

For Further Discussion

- Have you ever been afraid after you:
  - Made a major mistake?
  - Cheated on a test?
  - Lied to someone at work?
- Have you become jealous that someone else might get what you wanted?
- Do you now see things differently knowing what happened to Saul and what God really had in store for him? And for you?
- Did this story teach you how to truly be a friend to your peers and how you are to honor your father and mother, even when they are wrong?
- What can we learn from these two "brothers" (David and Jonathan)? Putting others ahead of yourself (our second lesson) does not feel natural; that is why we need to let God be in control. Do you see how God, through us, can do the things we cannot do on our own?

For Further Study

1. John 14:1, 27—Do not let your hearts be troubled; believe in God; believe also in Jesus. Jesus says, "Peace I leave with you; my peace I give you. I do not give to you as the world gives. Do not let your hearts be troubled and do not be afraid."
2. Philippians 2:3—Do nothing out of selfish ambition or vain conceit. Rather, in humility, value others above yourselves.
3. Philippians 2:5–10—In your relationships with one another, have the same mindset as Jesus. He chose to give up his divine powers (equality with God) and become human; further, he humbled himself by his willingness to die on a cross. Therefore, God exalted him to the highest place and gave him the name that is above every name, that at the name of Jesus every knee should bow, in heaven and on earth and under the earth.
4. Romans 8:28—God works all things for good for those who love him, who have been called according to his purpose.
5. Romans 12:10—Be devoted to one another in love. Honor one another above yourselves.

Chapter 23

DAVID FLEES FROM THE WRATH OF SAUL

1 Samuel 21–24, 26

From previous stories, we know David was anointed king of Israel by God. However, Saul was still ruler, and David decided, since God made Saul king, he would let God decide when it was time for him (David) to reign. In the meantime, David had to flee; otherwise, Saul would have had him killed. While many knew Saul was after David, many others only knew how great a military leader David was and how loyal he was to Saul.

David Finds Help along the Way

Many important people helped David along the way. A priest named Ahimelech gave David bread to eat and offered him the sword of Goliath that had been given to the priest for safekeeping. Soon, David left the territory of Israel and escaped into a neighboring kingdom; however, because he was so well-known, the king in this enemy territory was ready to seize David. To avoid capture, David acted like a madman, with foam coming out of his mouth, so the king let him go.

David became like a nomad, continually looking for places to hide. Sometimes he lived in caves with very little to eat, and other times he went into neighboring kingdoms to find refuge. People quickly learned of David's plight, and those closest to David joined him, including his father and mother, brothers, and three nephews, who fought under David's command. They, too, needed to escape the king's wrath. In addition, those who were in distress, in overwhelming debt, or generally displeased at the status of their life sought out David, who became their leader. The number of David's followers started out at four hundred and eventually grew to six hundred.

David's band of family, friends, misfits, and fugitives followed him throughout the time he spent hiding from Saul. Most of these men later became leaders in David's army after he was crowned king of Israel. However, David left his father and mother in the land of Moab, where he asked his friend, the king of Moab, to take care of them until his troubles with Saul could be resolved. You may recall that David's great-grandmother was a Moabite, which may explain David's friendship with this king.

How could God allow his anointed king to be treated as an outcast and exiled from his home? Our trials and tribulations teach us perseverance, which builds character. Through these difficulties, we have hope that God will come through in the end.[1] Christian hope comes with the *expectation* that we will receive what we are hoping for.[2] Because of what we learn during our trying and challenging times, we become useful to God. David's life is an example of this hope realized, and this becomes the **third lesson** in becoming disciplined and under God's control: **persevere through the trials and tribulations of life with the expectation (hope) that God will see you through them.**

In the meantime, Saul searched tirelessly for David. Saul was now paranoid and feared everyone was against him. He was upset that no one told him about the covenant Jonathan and David made together. He claimed no one in his kingdom was willing to help him defeat David.

When Saul confronted Ahimelech, the priest tried to explain that he was only helping a faithful servant of Saul and knew nothing of the hostility between the two. But Saul was not willing to hear him out and had Ahimelech and the other priests who were with him killed. One son of Ahimelech, Abiathar, escaped and fled to tell David what Saul had done. David felt responsible for the death of Ahimelech and the other priests; consequently, he agreed to keep Abiathar with him for safekeeping.

Saul is a good example of how lost we can become when we are concerned mainly with ourselves and our own self-interests. He was acting foolishly, similar to a mad man on the loose. Instead of enjoying what God had given him, he spent the rest of his life fighting evil spirits and pursuing David. All joy was taken from Saul because of his own actions and attitude.

Choosing God to Be in Control of Our Lives

In spite of Saul's feelings toward David, David continued to honor Saul as the king of Israel. Instead of fighting Saul, David ran from him. Even though God anointed David as king, he was willing to be subservient to Saul; so, under these circumstances, David was willing to be meek and humble, which, in God's world, means surrendering all to him. However, the world views meekness as weakness because it appears that others are taking advantage of the meek person. But in reality, meekness shows strength when the meek person makes the choice to submit. A person cannot take advantage of you if you knowingly allow the event or action to take place. You are meek, but not weak, when you submit to God and allow him to be in control.

When Jesus was arrested by the Jewish Council, his disciples were ready to fight, and they expected Jesus to take control. However, he responded, "Don't you know that I could ask my Father to call twelve legions of angels to help? But, it is not to happen that way."[3] While it appeared to the world his enemy was taking advantage of him, Jesus was accomplishing his earthly purpose and was able to save all who choose to accept him as their Lord and Savior.

Therefore, **be willing to surrender all to God**, which is the **fourth lesson** in becoming disciplined and under God's control. In the first lesson, we learned that God is sovereign, and we must accept or acknowledge that God is who he says he is. Now we learn that surrendering all to God's control is a process. As we grow in our relationship with God, we continually recognize new things we must surrender to God, and at times, we must submit to others under God's direction. When we choose to do it our way, we are likely to follow Saul's path. In contrast, once we are willing to surrender, we find ourselves on David's path to righteousness, where we are sure to face life's trials and tribulations. However, with God guiding us and leading the way, we can have peace and security.[4] The rewards only God can give will be ours.[5]

Jonathan, like David, was also willing to surrender all. When Jonathan learned Saul was pursuing David, he felt the need to encourage David. However, his visit was not without danger and the fear of Saul finding out. If Jonathan had been caught, Saul may have punished him, or Saul may have had Jonathan followed to capture David. When Jonathan found David, he reassured him,

> *Do not be afraid because the hand of my father will not find you. You will be king, and I will stand next to you.*

Wow! What a friend. This encouragement is just what David needed. Remember, Jonathan had every right to be king and was strong enough to fend off anyone who tried to take the throne from him, including David. But Jonathan chose to serve both God and David. He knew God's anointing was on David and was comfortable being under his friend's leadership. This meeting would be the last time Jonathan and David saw each other. As we learn in a later story, Jonathan would be killed with his father in battle and, therefore, not able to fulfill his dream of being David's right-hand man.

This story reminds me of how John the Baptist proclaimed that he must decrease so that Jesus may increase. It may be that God could not let Jonathan's presence prevent David from standing alone as king. Just as John the Baptist was very popular and would have detracted from Jesus' ministry, so too, Jonathan's popularity and position as Saul's son could have weakened David's rule and subjected his future sons to a threat of being overthrown. Only one ruler can be king. Just as the Israelites needed to choose David—and only David—as God's earthly king, we need to choose Jesus—and only Jesus—as God's heavenly king.

Each time Saul got close to catching David, he found a way to escape. Once, when Saul had David cornered, the Philistines attacked Israel, and Saul had to leave to protect his country. While the Bible does not specifically say, I am sure that God led the Philistines to attack at that precise moment to save David from Saul.

David had to watch his back every hour, not only from an attack by Saul but also from attack by anyone in the kingdom who wanted Saul's approval. The Philistines would have loved to kill David as revenge for all of the battles he won against them. But in spite of all these adversaries, David knew God was with him, and he was constantly going to God in prayer. For example, David asked God if he should go into battle against the Philistines to protect the town of

Keilah. When God told him yes, David led his men in victory. When he found out that Saul knew he was in Keilah, David asked God if the town's people would turn him over to Saul. When God told him yes, he left without any complaint. If I had just saved a town from its enemy, I would have expected a little more help from the citizens. What about you?

This is twice David sought God's direction and twice God gave him the answer. This becomes a **fifth lesson** in giving control to God: **spend time with God, getting to know him and seeking his wise counsel**. If David did not have a close relationship with God, he would not have been able to hear God's instruction.

God promises to be with us, but he does not promise a problem-free life. God wants us to learn how to deal with our problems, not expect him to solve them all for us. And too, we are called to suffer for God at times—even if we suffer through no fault of our own.[6]

The Caves of Engedi

We continue to learn that David did not follow the path most of us would pursue. David believed he would take over in God's time; therefore, he would not take matters into his own hands by trying to kill Saul. In fact, David would do just the opposite. No better example exists than what took place in the caves of Engedi.

While Engedi is a beautiful place to visit, it would be a very tough place to live. Engedi is a small mountain range in the middle of the desert with a series of

waterfalls, beautiful greenery, and small trees. It is an oasis of sorts, but it is no place I would want to live. However, David and his six hundred men took refuge with their families in the musty, dusty, and dark caves of the Engedi mountains.

When Saul discovered David was living in Engedi, he was pleased because he believed he could corner David in the mountains and finally capture him. However, there were too many caves and places to hide, so eventually Saul was ready to give up the search. Before he left, Saul went into one of the caves to relieve himself. By coincidence—perhaps a "holy coincidence" or divine intervention—Saul went into the very cave where David and some of his men were hiding. As Saul squatted, one of David's men whispered, "God has delivered your enemy into your hand."

If I had been David in that cave, I would have surely thought God was delivering me from all the trials and tribulations I had faced and that it was now time for me to be king. It would mean no more running, hiding, being hungry, or living in nasty conditions. It would mean finally enjoying a life of luxury as a king.

Besides, hadn't God anointed David as king? Hadn't he always been loyal to Saul? Hadn't he stayed away and let Saul have his kingdom? And it truly seemed as if God had now delivered Saul right into his hands. Certainly, he should be able to defend himself against a man who was out to kill him. So, David took out his knife and quietly crawled over to Saul while the king was in this uniquely vulnerable situation. But instead of killing Saul, David cut off the hem of his robe as proof that he had the opportunity to kill him but did not take advantage of it. Saul did not even notice what happened.

Only if you knew God very, very well could you have known it was *not* God's plan for David to kill Saul in this cave. David wanted God to give him the kingdom; he did not want to take it from Saul. He was truly listening to and following God. Though it requires a great deal of humility and restraint, these stories have shown that putting others ahead of your own needs[7] and surrendering all to God are keys to serving him. Unfortunately, we often think of ourselves first, but God tells us to be like Jesus by putting others first and allowing him to take care of us.[8] These lessons are resources God wanted David to discover before he became king. There are still more lessons to learn.

As Saul climbed down the mountain, David came out of the cave and shouted, "My lord, the king." Saul looked up to see David, who bowed with his face to the ground in honor to the king. David spoke,

Why do you listen to the words of men? Behold, I mean you no harm. This day, your eyes have seen that the Lord gave you into my hand. My men said I should kill you. But I responded that I will not stretch out my hand against

my lord, for he is the Lord's anointed. Now see, I have the edge of your robe in my hand. Since I did not kill you, can't you see that I intend no harm to you, though you are lying in wait to take my life? . . . Let the Lord be the judge between you and me that he may deliver me.

Saul wept and spoke,

You are more righteous than me. While I intend you harm, you have treated me well. May the Lord reward you for what you have done this day. Now behold, I know that you shall surely be king. Accordingly, I ask you to swear that you will not cut off my descendants after me.

David readily agreed to Saul's request. Wouldn't it be great if the story ended here? Sadly, Saul was only sorry for the moment. You may recall from earlier stories that being truly sorry requires a commitment not to do the wrong again. The Bible calls this repentance.[9] Unfortunately for Saul, as soon as he returned home, the evil spirits entered him, and he once again sought ways to capture David.

Who Should Be King?

Sometime later, David would once again spare the life of Saul. Saul was pursuing David when the people of Ziph told him David was in their territory.

While Saul was camping in the valley, David and his nephew Abishai snuck into the king's camp and had the opportunity to take Saul's own sword and kill him while he and his army slept. Abishai offered to kill Saul for David, but David said, "Surely, the Lord will strike him down, or his day will come that he dies, or he will be killed in battle by his enemy." That is, Saul's death and David's turn to be the king was fully in God's hands. Can we learn to surrender all to God in this same way? If only we could, our lives would be rich and rewarding.

So, who should be king? The answer is not so clear. God's Spirit was no longer with Saul, and he no longer considered Saul king of his people. For this reason, God sent Samuel to David's home to anoint him as the new king years earlier—even before David killed Goliath. Yet, David believed Saul was to remain king until God took the position from Saul. And too, the Israelites still honored Saul as king. David was prepared to patiently wait on God's timing. This brings us to the **sixth lesson** in giving up control to God: **be patient and wait on God's timing**.[10]

Can you imagine how David must have felt? It takes a lot of discipline to continue to struggle with life's trials and tribulations when you know one small act on your behalf would end your troubles, making all you want yours for the taking. But when we live by God's standards, we are to follow his lead—even if that means suffering while we patiently wait on his plans, just as David did in this story or as Joseph did years earlier living in the dungeon, though he had done nothing wrong, or as Jesus did for all of us when he suffered and died on the cross so that we may be saved from the punishment for our sins. Once we choose God, we will find—just as Joseph, David, and Jesus discovered—all blessings will come to us in God's time. How great the reward will be! How great the victory![11]

For Further Discussion

- Have your friends ever helped you even if it meant they would get in trouble? What should you do when this happens? How would you try to help a friend?
- Have you ever been out of control? Did you do something you now regret? How can you prevent this from happening again?
- What did you learn from David's willingness to forego killing Saul when he was given multiple opportunities?

- Describe what you think being disciplined and under God's control means. Does it include suffering, even when you have done nothing wrong?

For Further Study

1. Romans 5:3–5—Suffering produces perseverance; perseverance produces character; and character results in hope; and hope does not disappoint because God has given us the Holy Spirit as a promise.

2. Romans 4:16–20—Faith in God's grace guarantees the promise of salvation. "In hope against hope" (meaning Abraham had hope that God would deliver, even though from a worldly view it was impossible), God called into existence that which did not exist (a son for Abraham and Sarah), and through this hope we, too, can be fully assured of what God has promised. He is able to deliver. (Also see Romans 8:24–30.)

3. Matthew 26:53-54—Jesus let his disciples know that if he asked his Father, he would send twelve legions of angels to help, but that was not God's plan.

4. Trials and tribulations produce perseverance, and through it all, God gives us peace that exceeds our ability to understand:
   a. James 1:2–4—Consider it pure joy, my brothers and sisters, whenever you face trials of many kinds because you know that the testing of your faith produces perseverance. Let perseverance finish its work so that you may be mature and complete, not lacking anything.
   b. Philippians 4:7—The peace of God, which surpasses all comprehension, will guard your hearts and your minds in Christ Jesus.

5. 1 Corinthians 3:10–14—If our foundation is laid with our belief in Jesus, the works we build in this life will be rewarded by God.

6. 1 Peter 4:12–14—Do not be surprised at the fiery ordeal that has come on you to test you, as though something strange were happening to you. But rejoice inasmuch as you participate in the sufferings of Christ so that you may be overjoyed when his glory is revealed. If you are insulted in this world because of the name of Christ, you will one day receive bountiful rewards from God.

7. Philippians 2:3—Do nothing out of selfish ambition or vain conceit. Rather, in humility, value others above yourselves.

8. Matthew 6:24–26—Therefore, I tell you, do not worry about your life, what you will eat or drink, or about your body, what you will wear. Is not life more than food and the body more than clothes? Look at the birds of the air; they do not sow or reap or store away in barns, and

yet your heavenly Father feeds them. Are you not much more valuable than they?

9. 2 Corinthians 7:9—After Paul criticized the church at Corinth, he tells the people that he now rejoices, not that he made them sorrowful but that he made them sorrowful to the point of repentance.

10. Wait patiently on God's timing:

    a. Romans 8:24–30—Hope that is seen is no hope at all. Who hopes for what they already have? But if we hope for what we do not yet have, we wait for it patiently.

    b. 2 Thessalonians 1:4–5—We boast about your perseverance and faith in all the persecutions and trials you are enduring. All this is evidence that God's judgment is right, and as a result, you will be counted worthy of the kingdom of God, for which you are suffering.

11. 1 Corinthians 15:57—Thanks be to God! He gives us the victory through our Lord, Jesus Christ.

Chapter 24

DAVID'S LIFE ON THE RUN

1 Samuel 25

We have already learned about several of David's predicaments where he was forced to escape from Saul's wrath—but there's more. God was preparing David to lead his kingdom. From the struggles David faced, he would learn how the common people lived. While it is not the way the world would prepare a king, it is God's way—much like the life Joseph lived after his brothers sold him into slavery.[1] Learning to be humble and learning to be a servant is the way to achieve leadership in God's kingdom. Jesus was our perfect example; he is our king, yet he told his disciples that he came to serve and not to be served.[2] He gave up his powers and his equality with God to become a human, which led to his suffering and dying on the cross to save us from the punishment for our sins.[3]

Our **seventh lesson** in becoming disciplined and under God's control is learning to **live by the rules of heaven (God's world/kingdom), not those of the earth**. God's rules are much different than the rules our world (Satan's kingdom) teaches. In the "Tower of Babel" story from Volume 1, I shared that Peter said we, as believers, should act as aliens and strangers in this world;[4] Paul likewise told us that our citizenship is in heaven.[5] We are to put others before ourselves[6] and pray for those who persecute us, and if someone hits you on your cheek, allow him to slap the other cheek.[7] These commands do not seem right because the world we live in has taught us the wrong way for so many years. And too, our natural inclination is to put ourselves first and fight back. However, in the last few stories I've shared, David has demonstrated what it looks like to live by the rules of heaven, and we will continue to see his example over the next few stories.

Soon after Saul left Engedi, Samuel died, and all of Israel mourned for him. Samuel had been serving God since his early childhood. He first became the nation's leading priest, then their judge and protector. And finally, much like John the Baptist did when Jesus came forward with his ministry, Samuel ushered in the new system of government in Israel as he helped establish the monarchy, first through the selection of Saul and then David.

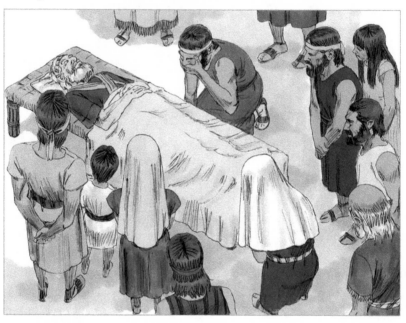

David Is Forced to Move On

As much as he wanted to attend Samuel's funeral, David could not, for Saul would have immediately captured him. Instead, David escaped to the desert south of Hebron, a major city in Judah. Nabal, a very rich man, lived in the region with his beautiful wife, Abigail. David helped protect Nabal's shepherds and their sheep from others who might be roaming the vast lands required to feed his three thousand sheep. After a time, David sent word to Nabal that he would appreciate a kind expression of thanks in the form of much-needed food and supplies for his men. However, Nabal was a selfish, evil man who scoffed at David's request and insulted him by questioning his integrity.

David was furious and prepared his men for a fight. Fortunately for David—and Nabal, too—Abigail got word of what Nabal had done. Not only was Abigail beautiful, but she was also intelligent and wise. Nabal's shepherds shared with Abigail how well David and his men had protected them the entire time they were out in the fields. These shepherds knew how upset David was and that he planned to seek revenge. And too, they knew how hardheaded and worthless their master was.

Abigail took it upon herself to gather enough bread, wine, meat, and fruits to feed David and his followers; then she ordered her servants to deliver this food before David reached her home. But she did not tell her husband what she was doing. When she met David on his way to seek revenge, he was still very angry. He told her that he was insulted by Nabal as he had returned David's good deeds with evil, so payback would not end until every male who belonged to Nabal was dead.

Clearly, David was out of control. This is not the David we have seen thus far. He was like many of us who finally break when we can stand it no more; Nabal's selfish refusal was "the straw that broke the camel's back." With so many people taking advantage of him, David got tired of it, and this latest rejection caused him to reach his limit. Even though Nabal's servants had not done anything to David, he was going to take out his frustrations on them.

Abigail Saves the Day

When Abigail saw David, she bowed before him and pleaded with him to listen to her. She tried to take the blame. She did not try to defend her worthless husband; rather, she told David that if she had known of his request, she would have gladly complied. She affirmed what a great man David was and testified that he was serving God in a mighty way; she knew he was destined to become king of Israel and reminded him that exacting revenge on Nabal was not worth having a blight on his record.

Further, she was concerned that evil may take hold of him if he started down this path. It was not like David to seek revenge, even though Nabal deserved it. Abigail did not want David's greatness to be overshadowed by shedding blood of innocent servants. She implored David to take her gifts as a thank you for the protection his men provided and as a reward for not taking revenge on a worthless man.

Boy, was David impressed! He said to her,

Blessed be the Lord God of Israel who sent you this day to meet me and blessed be your discernment. Thank you for stopping me from doing this foolish act of bloodshed and damaging my own reputation. Surely, if you had not come, I would have completed my revenge until all the male servants of Nabal were dead.

David accepted her gracious gift of food and told her to go in peace and know that he had listened to her wise words. In this story, we learn of another great truth of God: "Give and it will be given to you; your gift will be repaid in good measure, pressed down and running over."[8] Surely David was repaid for his protection, but the actions of Abigail provide the real truth of the lesson we must learn. The key here is that she did it because it was the right thing to do—not because she expected something in return. As you will see at the end of this story, God repaid her with a gift of his own, much more than Abigail could have ever imagined. You cannot out give God.

This brings us to our **eighth lesson** in becoming disciplined and under God's control: **seek and listen to the wise counsel of others**. God may place another person in our lives to set us back on the right path. There will be times in this life where we may lose control, and our ability to listen to God may be weak. When we are tempted to head in the wrong direction, it might just be that we need someone to confront us regarding our actions. Abigail was much like an angel of mercy; she was wise and generous, appealing to the goodness within David and preventing him from committing an act he would later regret. From Abigail, David learned a lesson in humility and meekness (not being weak but having the strength of character to allow God to help him control his emotions and reactions). God will send others into our lives to help us in our quest to stay under his control.

God Takes Control

So, what was Nabal doing all this time? He was with his friends having a party fit for a king. He was so drunk that Abigail did not bother to tell him about her meeting with David until the next morning. When she did, "his heart died within him so that he became as a stone" (this has been interpreted to mean he was paralyzed). Ten days later, God caused Nabal to have a stroke, and he died.

When David heard the news, he was thankful that he listened to the wise counsel of Abigail. God had taken revenge for David; he did not have to regret his actions against the innocent men of Nabal's household, yet he was still avenged. What a great lesson we can learn. Anger will cause us to do things we should not. We must allow God to teach us and share with us what he wants us to do. At times, he will tell us to let it go, and he will take care of the problem for us. Perhaps not as quickly as he did with Nabal, but we can have confidence that God will exact revenge for us in his perfect timing.

David immediately sent his servants to invite Abigail to become his wife. Because she had great respect and appreciation for who David was, she gladly accepted the offer of marriage. Also remember, she had already prophesied that David would become king of Israel. So, while there could be a rough road ahead, she expected that one day she would be part of the royal family. Now we learn even more about God in Abigail's story. She became a servant of God by delivering the message that prevented David from committing an evil act, and she was rewarded with becoming his wife. It is interesting to note that Michal, David's wife given by Saul, remained in the palace; we are not told whether David knew it, but Saul had given her to another man in marriage. While it was David who

asked Abigail to marry him, it was God who struck Nabal dead and provided the opportunity for the marriage. Abigail was paid back much more than she gave—pressed down and running over. She ultimately became the wife of the king of Israel.

Unfortunately, this world has taught us that submission is demeaning and wrong. In fact, "submission" is perceived to be a dirty word in today's culture. I believe Satan has intentionally caused this shift to prevent us from getting close to God. Satan's strongest desire is to keep us from deepening our relationship with God and with each other. We want to be independent. We ask, "Why do I have to do what my boss tells me when I do not agree? I should be able to do it my way!" In this world, it is all about *me*. Burger King's slogan for many years has been, "Have it *your* way." And the cosmetic company L'Oréal says, "Because *you're* worth it." Advertisers know how to exploit our selfish tendencies.

In contrast, Abigail and David depict a portrait of the church and Christ[9] as bride and Bridegroom.[10] Submit to Jesus, and you will be a ruler with him in his kingdom forever. Submit to those in authority, first to God and then to those God has put over you. In God's world, you are part of the royal family.

For Further Discussion

- Can you think of ways God's rules are different from the world's rules? Why should we live our life according to God's standards, rather than the way the world has taught us?
- David had a right to be upset with Nabal, so why was Abigail's suggestion better than what David had planned?
- Why was it a good idea for Abigail to be submissive before David?
- How will this story cause you to act differently when bad and unfair things happen to you?

For Further Study

1. Genesis 37:26–28, 36—Joseph's brothers were so jealous of him that they sold him to the Midianites, who sold him to Potiphar; Joseph then served Potiphar as his slave.

2. Matthew 20:25–28—This world says slaves must serve masters, but Jesus, our King, says he came to serve, *not* to be served. The greatest in his kingdom is the person who serves.

3. Philippians 2:5–9—Jesus gave up his godly powers to become a man and die on the cross to save us.

4. 1 Peter 2:11–12—Peter urges us to be aliens and strangers in this world, which means we realize this world has a different set of rules than those God calls us to live by. If we act as God has called us to, we will be witnesses for God. We must recognize that this world will not agree with the way we live.

5. Philippians 3:20—Paul plainly states that our citizenship is in heaven, not here on earth, which helps to explain 1 Peter 2:11–12: we are aliens and strangers while we live on earth.

6. Philippians 2:3–4—Treat each other as more important than yourself; look out for others.

7. Luke 6:27–29—We need to pray for our enemies and bless those who persecute us; if someone slaps us once, we should let him do it again, rather than fight back.

8. Luke 6:38—The more you give, the more God will give to you. Understand that if you give just to get something in return, it will not happen, but if you give from your heart, then God will bless you in ways you would never imagine.

9. Ephesians 5:23, 25—The husband is the head of the wife as Jesus is the head of the church; husbands are to love their wives as Jesus loves the church and was willing to die for the church.

10. Revelation 19:7:21:2, 9—The church (the body of Christ) represents the bride and Jesus (the lamb) is the Bridegroom.

Chapter 25

DAVID'S LIFE IN THE LAND OF HIS ENEMY

1 Samuel 27–30

What was next for David? As I shared in a previous story, Saul continued to pursue David, even though he knew David had twice resisted opportunities to kill him. Each time David departed, he told Saul that he wished they could come back together. However, that was not to be; therefore, David left the territory of Israel feeling lost from his homeland.

David in Philistia

Where did David go? He chose to enter enemy territory and went to Philistia. If he could convince the Philistines that he had been exiled from his home, he believed they would take him in. Saul could not enter into the stronghold of the enemy, so David hoped his family could live in Philistia more comfortably than in the desert. Yet David fought and won many victories against this enemy, so how would they receive him? Would they try to kill him?

The Philistines had five territories, each ruled by its own king with its own major city. While I am sure the Philistines had disputes among themselves, they bound together in times of war. David was able to negotiate a deal with the king of Gath's son, Achish. Achish knew about the trouble between Saul and David; therefore, he determined that as an enemy of Saul, David would be a friend to the Philistines.

During his time in Philistia, David raided neighboring countries but told Achish the raids were made in Israel. This behavior helped convince Achish that David's ties with his country were severed. As a result, Achish believed David would be his servant forever. When David agreed to go to war and help Achish, the king was ready to take David on as his body guard.

Life here on earth will not always follow the path we hope for. The Bible tells us that Jesus suffered for us, and as his soldiers, we, too, are expected to suffer. Thankfully, God promises to be with us, just like he was with David. David had done nothing wrong to deserve this kind of treatment from Saul. In fact, he had been a loyal subject, which resulted in great honor and victories for Saul and his kingdom. However, it appeared David's earthly reward was to be attacked and run out of his country; he was often left without food or shelter, living in caves or in the desert. And now, he was living subservient to his enemies.

Why would David be required to endure such hardship? As I have shared, our trials and tribulations on this earth provide us the opportunity to learn how to persevere. This was our third lesson in being disciplined and under God's control: perseverance develops our character so that we can become useful to God with the expectation (the Christian hope) of eternal life[1] with God, reigning with him as fellow heirs in Jesus' kingdom.[2] While accepting the trials this process may bring is not easy, in the end, it is wonderfully rewarding.

Saul Seeks Guidance in the Wrong Place

Sometime later, the Philistines geared up for battle against Israel. When Saul heard of the impending attack, he decided to consult a medium/spiritist, a person who claims to speak with the spirit world. Since God was no longer speaking to him, Saul felt compelled to talk with Samuel, who had recently died. Once again, Saul was going against God; however, this time his behavior also went against one of his own laws. Early in his reign, Saul pleased God by cleansing the land of spiritists who sought to speak to the spirit world rather than seeking God.

There are people today who claim to have access to the spiritual world. While I recognize that most spiritists are fakes, I do believe evil spirits (or demons and angels who have chosen to side with the devil) communicate with a limited number of spiritists. However, associating with spiritists (or psychics, as they are often referred to today) at best leads us away from God and will often end in trouble. We must trust that God knows best and stay away from anyone practicing these evil acts.[3]

More important, we need to learn that God will communicate to us from the spiritual world, but in his way—not in the way of "spiritists." As an example, God may send an angel as a messenger, as he regularly did in the Old Testament stories, but most often he speaks directly to our heart and mind through the Holy Spirit who lives inside all who believe Jesus is their Lord and Savior (believers).[4]

Now, back to the story. Saul was disguised so that no one would discover what he was doing. The spiritist Saul found was frightened and did not want to help this stranger who asked her to break the law. But she agreed to help after he threatened her. And in this unusual and very limited circumstance, God allowed Samuel to speak through the spiritist. When she realized it was Samuel with whom she was speaking, she also realized it was Saul who made the request. Then she really got scared and feared for her life.

Samuel was upset with Saul for disturbing him and said if God would not answer him, he should have known it would be bad news. Samuel told Saul, "Tomorrow, you and your sons will be with me, and David will become king of Israel." This prophesy from the dead was devastating news to Saul. He collapsed as the years of fighting against God and David overwhelmed him. The spiritist and Saul's men got him to rest and take some food. This helped a bit, and Saul returned home; afterwards, he headed to the battlefield, hoping somehow, he could circumvent Samuel's prediction.

Did Samuel come back from the dead? Where had he been? Where would Saul be after his death? Samuel did not come back to life; God allowed Samuel's spirit to give Saul his answer. I shared in an earlier story that Sheol (the Greek word is "Hades") was the place where a person's spirit went after death. In Sheol, there was a place of peace and joy for those who believed and trusted in God (sometimes the Bible refers to this place as "paradise"), with a separate place of punishment for the non-believer.[5]

For sure, Jonathan would be with Samuel in paradise. What about Saul? We are not given anything specific to make a determination. But this is how I see it: Saul was a believer who got lost along the way. His own selfish interest and love for himself outweighed what he knew was right. Jesus died for our sins, for those who lived before him and for those who lived after. We do not get to "heaven" based on our own merits; it is Jesus' life's work completed at the cross when he rose from the dead and earned the right to offer us salvation. Therefore, we cannot "sin" our way into hell if we have accepted God's gift of salvation through Jesus and neither could Saul. He was a believer who made a lot of mistakes. Even so, I believe he fits into the "saved but lost rewards" category described by Paul in I Corinthians, where he says those whose foundations are built on Jesus Christ will be saved through the fire, but those who built little or nothing on the foundation will lose rewards in the next life.[6]

Difficult Choices in Difficult Times

In the meantime, Achish's fellow kings did not believe David was on their side and would not allow him to go into battle with them. They remembered the battle with Goliath and the songs the Israelites sang: "David killed his ten thousands." Achish argued that David had been his faithful servant for over a year; further, he deserted his homeland and was clearly an enemy of Saul. David had fooled Achish but not the others.

Achish told David the news. While he outwardly protested, I believe David was secretly very glad he would not be put in such a difficult position to fight against Saul and his fellow Israelites. The Philistines were very concerned that David would turn on them in the middle of the battle, and they were probably right. Certainly, David would not have killed his fellow countrymen. He already had two opportunities to kill Saul and chose not to do it. Would he now help his enemies in battle?

If he did, what kind of position would this have put David in? I believe this was a situation in which God intervened to protect David and his countrymen. Samuel had prophesied that Israel was going to lose this battle and that God was ready for David to be king. Therefore, this was not a good time to be associated with the enemy and thus lose favor with his people. David and Achish departed as friends—or so David allowed him to believe.

From this story we can learn that while God expects us to endure in the face of trials and tribulations, he will protect us—even when we cannot see it.

When David and his men returned to Gath, they discovered the Amalekites (another enemy) had taken their wives and children and stolen their possessions. The men were upset with David, but what would have happened if David and his army had been allowed to go into battle with the Philistines? They would not have been back in time to go after the enemy and rescue their families. Because of God's intervention, they were able to reclaim their families, retrieve their possessions, *and* claim the spoils the Amalekites had taken from quite a number of other cities.

The timing was just right. Even though they had not heard Samuel's prophecy, David and his men would be able to return to their homeland (Israel), taking their new-found riches with them. The wait was worth it. Many of these men originally came to David because they were in trouble and on the run. They, too, would be able to return home with their heads up, their troubles forgotten, and their crimes forgiven.

It is the same with us. God is so very gracious to look past our problems and faults and take us in as members of his family. He is prepared to make us rich beyond our understanding, with treasures such as joy, peace, kindness, self-control, patience, love, goodness, faithfulness, and gentleness;[7] and more important, we also have the promise of eternity with him. These riches are so much better than this world's material possessions. I am afraid too many of us will realize this truth too late. Learn to make an effort to do it God's way. And by turning from past troubles and mistakes, we will find God is there to forgive and forget, and he'll even be ready to share his blessing with us.[8]

Working Together for God

David's men still had much to learn. Some did not want to share the spoils of victory with those who had become too exhausted to continue after the enemy. As I just shared, many of David's men were outcasts, and a number of them had run away from their crimes at home. David had always done a good job of keeping them together and on the right track, so he would have none of this discussion. He said everyone was part of the team; everyone had a job to do, from small to large, and all would participate in the rewards of victory. This set a precedent. In David's kingdom, everyone would do his assigned part, whether small or large, and all would share in the spoils and rewards of victory. This is the **ninth lesson** in the quest to become disciplined and under God's control: **share your wealth and good fortune with your fellow human beings**. There is no place in God's kingdom for selfishness.

David let it be known to his men that each person had an important role to play. No one should think his job was more important than that of his countryman. This is true in God's kingdom as well: everyone has a role. In the New Testament, Paul gives an example, saying all believers are part of the body of Christ, each with an equally important function/job. Some people are the eyes of the body; some are the hands; and others are the toes. God wants each of us to perform the function we are given. If one member suffers, the whole body suffers. If one member is honored, all members receive honor.[9]

I am concluding the lessons in being disciplined and under God's control with this **tenth and final lesson: perform your specific role in God's kingdom**. God will reward each of us for what we do.[10] And what the world may perceive as "lesser" jobs are equally important to God and equally rewarding. In God's eyes, the usher's role is just as important in the church service as the preacher's role. This emphasizes God's plan for us to come together as a community of believers working to bring God's will on earth as it is in heaven, with each of us offering varying skills that help form the body of Christ, the church.

Each individual is rewarded based on how well the job is done, not based on the job given. Jesus gives us this lesson in the parable of the talents. The master told each servant who made a nice return on the talents he had been given,

Well done, my good and faithful servant, you have been faithful with a few things, I will now put you in charge of many; enter into the joy of your master.[11]

The master was happy with the return each servant made and did not distinguish between how much more one servant made over another. Both servants were told "well done." But to the one who hid his talent and gave nothing in return, the master was terribly upset and took the talent away from him.[12] Since this parable was intended to demonstrate what is expected from us for the talents we receive, let's make a supreme effort to serve God by using the gifts given us. In the end, the honor and glory will be ours as we are given the privilege to serve as rulers in eternity with Jesus.[2]

For Further Discussion

- Why do you think God delayed so long in giving the kingdom to David?
- Have you heard of someone visiting a spiritist, a person who claims to hear and talk to the dead? Why would God say this is wrong?
- Have you ever found yourself in a circumstance you did not know how to get out of but then somehow found resolution so you did not have to deal with the problem? Have you ever considered that God may have intervened and resolved the problem for you?

- Why do you think God wants us to share with our fellow Christians? Do you see how we are all equal in God's eyes?
- God has given each of us talents to help him in the work of his kingdom. The parable of the talents (money given to the servants to invest) tells us that God expects something in return for these talents. What are your talents? How can you use them to advance God's kingdom forward?

For Further Study

1. Romans 5:3–5—Trials and tribulations develop perseverance, which builds character and leads to the hope of eternal life with Jesus.
2. Romans 8:16–17—Once we are a believer in Jesus, we become a child of God; as a child of God, we are joint-heirs with Jesus.
3. Exodus 22:18; Deuteronomy 18:10–11—The Law of Moses provides guidance for our view of spiritists: "You shall not allow a sorceress to live"; "There shall not be found among you one who . . . uses divination, one who practices witchcraft . . . or one who casts a spell . . . or a spiritist or one who calls up the dead."
4. The following passages share ways God speaks to us from his world:
   a. Romans 8:11—Jesus gives life to our mortal bodies through the Holy Spirit, who lives in you.
   b. John 16:7, 13—When Jesus left our world, he sent the Holy Spirit to guide us into all truths. The Holy Spirit will share only what Jesus and the Father tell him to.
   c. Hebrews 8:10—God declares that he will put his laws into our minds and will write them on our hearts.
   d. 1 Corinthians 14:1–3, 29–31—God gives the gift of prophesy to believers who are to share the message from God for the edification (building up) of the body of Christ (members of the church).
   e. Acts 5:19–20—An angel of God came to Peter and John and opened the prison gates and instructed them to speak God's Word in the temple.
   f. I Corinthians 3:16—Do you not know your body is a temple of the Holy Spirit?
5. Luke 16:22–25—When the poor man died, he went to Abraham's bosom (paradise); the rich man who had not shared with the poor man while he was alive went to a separate section in Hades where he was punished and in agony. He could see the poor man, but there was a chasm between them, with no help available for the rich man.

6. I Corinthians 3:10–15—All Christians have one thing in common: the belief that Jesus is the Son of God who died on the cross and rose on the third day to save us from punishment for our sins. We are all to be in service to him. Our works will be put to the test of fire. If any man's work is burned up, he will suffer loss, but he himself will be saved, yet so as through fire.

7. Galatians 5:22–23—The fruit of the Spirit is love, joy, peace, patience, kindness, goodness, faithfulness, gentleness, and self-control; against such things, there is no law.

8. Psalm 103:3, 8–12—Bless the Lord who forgives all my sins; the Lord is compassionate and slow to anger. For as high as the heavens are from the earth, so great is his loving kindness to those who fear him. He has removed our sins as far as the East is from the West.

9. 1 Corinthians 12:12–26—Paul explains that each church member is equally important. He compares the body of Christ (the church) with the various members of our physical body and asserts that each is equally important, from our eyes to our hands to our toes. All serve an important purpose and are equal in the eyes of God.

10. 1 Corinthians 3:14—To further elaborate on Luke 16:22–25, Paul shares, "If any man's work, which he has built on [his foundation], remains [through the fire], he will receive a reward."

11. Matthew 25:21—His master said to him, "Well done, good and faithful servant. You were faithful with a few things, so I will put you in charge of many things; enter into the joy of your master."

12. Matthew 25:14–30—Each servant was given money to invest for his master. After a time, the master came to the servants to see what each had done with the money given him. Each one who made at least some return on the money was blessed wonderfully by the master. The one who was so scared that he hid the money and did not even try to earn anything was condemned to be punished.

Chapter 26

DAVID, THE NEW KING OF ISRAEL

I Samuel 31 and 2 Samuel 1–2

In the previous story, Saul was very worried about the upcoming battle with the Philistines. He could not ask God what he should do because God was not speaking to him. So, Saul decided he would call on Samuel. Since Samuel had died a few years earlier, Saul would need to consult a spiritist; however, conferring with a spiritist was against both the will of God and Saul's own law. Surprisingly, it worked, but unfortunately for Saul, Samuel told him that he and his sons would soon die in battle. Saul hoped he could overcome this fate.

In the meantime, David was living in the land of the Philistines, but he was not allowed to fight with them. At the time of the battle, he had to save his own family from the hands of another enemy, which he and his men did with great success. If Saul and his sons were killed in battle, it would mean God was finally ready for David to become king.

Saul and Jonathan's Last Battle

Saul entered the battle arena at the famous battle site where Gideon led Israel against the Midianites many years earlier. Do you remember how God chose only three hundred men to fight with Gideon against 135,000 enemy soldiers and yet Israel won the battle?[1] This time it would not work out so well. The battle was going badly; Jonathan and two of his brothers were killed during the battle, and Saul was severely injured by the Philistine archers. He was afraid they would capture and torture him, so Saul asked his armor bearer to kill him. When the armor bearer would not, Saul decided to fall on his own sword and die. Because the armor bearer's job was to protect Saul, he felt he had failed and decided to fall on his sword and die with Saul.

The Philistines were so glad to eliminate these valiant foes that they hung the bodies of Saul and his sons up on the walls of one of their cities as a special victory celebration. While the remainder of Israel retreated in fear, some fearless men mustered their courage and stole the bodies of Saul, Jonathan, and Saul's other two sons from the Philistines. Israel came together to bury their fallen leaders and honored their memory by mourning for seven days.

David and his men were back in their home near Gath, waiting to hear the results of the battle between the Israelites and the Philistines. A man from Saul's camp arrived three days after the death of Saul to tell David the news. He was a slave and clearly thought that the death of Saul would be good news to David. He even claimed to have killed Saul, hoping David would honor him for this deed. He had stolen Saul's crown and bracelet from the battlefield where Saul was killed to show proof of his act. Apparently, he found Saul soon after he killed himself but before the Philistines discovered he was dead.

The slave, of course, did not know David at all. Instead of rejoicing, David and his men tore their clothes as a sign of sorrow and mourned for Saul, Jonathan, and the entire house of Israel. If you remember, David was a masterful musician. In memory of Saul and Jonathan, he wrote a song in the form of a lament called the "Song of the Bow."

Later that evening, David summoned the man who claimed to have killed Saul and said, "How is it that you were not afraid to kill the Lord's anointed? Your blood is on your own head." Then, David had one of his young men kill the slave. This is a tough lesson to learn. Here was a young man who died for something he did not do, but this was of his own making. David had no way of knowing that he was lying, for the slave even had Saul's crown and bracelet as proof he had killed him. I think David would have been equally upset to know that the man lied about this act just to get into his good graces.

If the slave had been more in tune with what was going on around him, he would have known how much David loved Saul, and especially Jonathan. He could have given him the horrible news with a grief-stricken attitude and offered the crown and bracelet to David for safe keeping. I believe this would have resulted in the slave being honored; and possibly invited to join David's army. This points out how important it is to be aware of our circumstances and surroundings. And even more so, of what is going on with God and his plans for us. When we are not in tune with God, we are likely to get in his way and become lost in the battle he has called us to join. That is why we do not want to close our eyes to things of this world; also, we need to become intimately familiar with the Bible and spend time in prayer and meditation to seek and know God's will for us and his plans for the world.[2]

David Returns to Israel and Becomes King

After the seven days of mourning ended, David inquired of the Lord, "Shall I go to one of the cities of Judah?" God told him, "Yes, go to the city of Hebron." Remember, David was a member of the tribe of Judah, and it is there David and his family settled with his army and all their families. Soon the men of Judah came to David and officially anointed him king over the tribe of Judah. Then, David sent messengers to thank the valiant men who rescued the bodies of Saul and Jonathan; he promised to treat them with kindness and goodness for their great action. And too, he let them know that he had been anointed king of Judah.

Can you see how wise David was? Yes, he was pleased with what these men had done, but too, he was setting himself up to get in good with them and to let them know he had been crowned king of Judah. This was a subtle way to invite them to make him king over all of Israel. As it turned out, they did not join with David right away, but it did make a good impression that would benefit him later. This reminds us that to live in this world, we need to follow the saying, "Be wise as foxes and gentle as lambs." Complimenting someone never hurts—especially when it is true. While you need to be careful that the compliment is sincere, it does not mean you cannot use it positively for your benefit.

David Is Disciplined and under God's Control

David was now ready to be king. Let's summarize how God had been training him with the **ten lessons** we have learned in the past several stories regarding becoming **disciplined and under God's control**:

1. **Give your life to God and recognize his sovereignty.** When David heard the taunts of Goliath against the Israelite God, he declared that no one could speak about the almighty God like that. And he, trusting God was in control, won against all odds, even against a giant the size of Goliath (chapter 21).

2. **Put the needs of others in front of your own.** Jonathan gave up his right to the throne to serve David (chapter 22).

3. **Persevere through trials and tribulations with the expectation (hope) that God will see you through.** David and his men had nowhere to go, and as they moved from place to place, they had to endure the rejection of others and live in the most horrible of circumstances, yet they endured with the hope (expectation) that God would deliver them in the end (chapter 23).

4. **Be willing to surrender all to God.** David was anointed king, but he chose to be subservient to Saul and let God choose the timing for him to take over the throne; even though there was much stress and hardship, David endured by choosing God's way (chapter 23).

5. **Spend time with God, getting to know him and seeking his counsel.** Twice David asked God what to do, and both times he followed God's advice. If he had not taken time to meditate and get to know his heavenly father, he would not have been able to recognize and hear God's voice (chapter 23).

6. **Be patient and wait on God's timing.** David is given two opportunities to kill Saul and take over the kingdom, but he decided the kingdom

must be received in God's timing. God was putting him to the test, and David passed with flying colors (chapter 23).

7. **Live by the rules of heaven (God's world/kingdom), not those of the earth.** David learned to live by God's rules, not the earthly laws established by Satan or the sinful nature of man (chapter 24).

8. **Seek and listen to the wise counsel of others.** When David's anger was about to get the best of him, Abigail saved David from committing the horrible act of killing the servants of Nabal (chapter 24).

9. **Share your wealth and good fortune with your fellow human beings.** Some of David's men were exhausted and could not continue after the enemy took their families, but David shared the spoils of victory with everyone (chapter 25).

10. **Perform your specific role in God's kingdom.** All members of David's team were equally valuable, with each member responsible to discover and perform the role God gave him. David established a rule: all members had jobs to do, and no job had more privileges than the others (chapter 25).

Teaching David through these ten lessons was God's way of preparing him to be king of his (God's) people. In the same way, God uses the lessons from these stories to share how we, too, need to live our lives and lead others. Yes, as members the body of Christ, we are called to be leaders and "bring God's kingdom on earth as it is in heaven."[3]

While the primary message in these ten lessons was David's development and preparation to be king, it is equally important for us to understand that God is sharing how we, too, need to prepare ourselves for his service. What would our church look like if we all followed this set of standards established by God? What could we accomplish? I think it would be an amazing thing to see. Harmony and peace would reign, and I believe we would then begin to infect the world with this same attitude. Life would be as God originally planned. Unfortunately, God says we will not see this until Jesus returns to be the ruler of the earth. What a glorious day that will be! Until then, we can perform the specific roles God has given each of us and thus begin the process of forming the body of Christ, the church.

While the devil still reigns here on earth, our citizenship is in heaven.[4] So we need to be under the rule of our King Jesus. We must follow his laws, take our needs before his throne, be prepared to listen to the messages he sends, and finally, follow all he says.

David is now ready to be king; more important, God is ready for David to be king. In the same way, if you are willing to be obedient, God will prepare you to be a leader in the church/body of Christ.

For Further Discussion

- Why does David always get upset when people deliver what they think is good news about his enemies? Does David see Saul and his sons as enemies? How do you view fellow Christians who have been mean or ugly to you?
- Why was it important for David to get in good with the supporters of Saul and Jonathan?
- Being disciplined and under God's control requires you to take on Jesus' yoke. What does this mean? Giving God control of your life is tough. How does this act of submission change how you will live your life?
- Which of the ten lessons in becoming disciplined and under God's control is hardest for you? Do you see that you have to be willing to obey all ten lessons to please God completely? How will you be blessed if you *strive* to believe and practice all of them?
- Spend some time envisioning how each lesson can be incorporated into your lifestyle.

For Further Study

1. Judges 7:1–8—God asked Gideon to take only three hundred men to fight the enemy army of 135,000 soldiers. God wanted all to know that it was he (God) who won the victory as three hundred men could not defeat an army of 135,000 without God's intervention.
2. Matthew 6:33—Seek first [Jesus'] kingdom and his righteousness, and all the things you need will be added to you.
3. Matthew 6:10 – God's kingdom come, his will be done, on earth as it is in heaven.
4. Philippians 3:20—Our citizenship is in heaven, which helps to explain why Jesus told us that the devil is the ruler of this world. (Also see John 12:31; 14:30.)

WHAT'S NEXT?

Volume 3 of the *Making God Part of Your Family* series will concentrate on David and his descendants (the kings of God's Chosen Family) as well as the prophets who delivered God's messages and his Word. We will learn how after two years, David secured all of Israel under his control. As a result, peace and harmony was the general rule among God's people. However, David and the kings that followed him became proud of these accomplishments—a little too proud. This is often the case when things are going well for us.

Over the next three hundred years, the stories will show how these kings and the Chosen Family turned away from God over and over again. But when they cried for help, God allowed great kings and great men to rise up and lead God's people. For a while things would be good, until the pleasures and temptations of this world turned the Israelites' focus away from God.

Finally, God's family became hopelessly lost. God allowed them to be taken captive to a foreign land where they ultimately understood and acknowledged what it meant to serve the one and only true God. Eventually, they were allowed to return to the Promised Land to rebuild the Temple and Jerusalem. And that is where the history of the Old Testament ends. Between the time when the recorded history of the Old Testament ends and the New Testament begins, the worship of God alone is firmly established.

But even then, the Chosen Family could not fully submit to God; the leaders worshiped their own rules and selfish desires. The descendants of Adam (mankind) would never be able to reconcile themselves to God without his help due to their sinful nature. At last, God was ready to send his Son, Jesus, to rescue us. And that is where the New Testament begins.

221

In the next volume, I will continue to illustrate the parallels of Old Testament stories to our world today. For example, at times in American history, we have seen great men rise up and lead the country to new heights. But then we become arrogant and boastful; we stumble and fall. We have much more to learn from the teachings of God's Old Testament Word.

I hope you will continue to follow with me through Volume 3 as I share what happens to David and his descendants. Hopefully, we will learn new lessons presented through the remaining Old Testament stories and be wise enough to avoid the pitfalls that so easily ensnare us.

ABOUT THE AUTHOR

During his professional career as a CPA, Michael Grady acted primarily as a trusted advisor and along the way became an experienced educator and professional speaker. As a result, he has written and presented numerous continuing education courses, college courses, and marketing presentations.

While he has had a successful business career, Michael will tell you that his Christian ministry is the more important aspect of his life. In the same way that Paul made tents to earn a living, Michael offers financial and business advice to others, which often provides him an opportunity to share his faith. He is father to one son and one daughter, proud grandfather of three, and presently lives with his wife, Nan, in Florence, South Carolina.

Michael has taught Sunday school and Bible study groups to all ages (adults, elementary children, and teenagers) for over thirty years. He continues to be a guest speaker in multiple churches, a certified lay speaker within the United Methodist Church, and leader of the Second Mile Evangelistic Association. Thus, he is very comfortable speaking on a variety of Christian topics.

Michael is available to speak at churches, schools, or special Christian events. He has a team that can coordinate a Sunday event or an entire weekend of Bible teachings for all ages, complete with worship services filled with music and testimonies.

This series of books has been a desire of Michael's for over twenty-five years. Through his years of teaching, he discovered that very few people have even a basic knowledge of the Bible. To help Christians learn outside of Sunday morning services, he designed this study book in story form. These volumes illuminate biblical messages that provide both practical benefits for our daily lives and eternal rewards for all who believe the good news of Jesus.

For more information, please visit Michael's ministry website at www.michaelgrady.org or e-mail him at michael@michaelgrady.org.